Historical Connections i[n]

Table of Cont[ents]

INTRODUCTION 7

CHAPTER 1
Portrait of Eratosthenes (c. 276 - c.195 B.C.) 9
Eratosthenes: The Earth Measurer 10
Activities:
    The Sieve of Eratosthenes 12
    Prime Magic 13
    Is it Always True? 14
    Odds in the Making 15
    The Earth and the Wire Belt 16

CHAPTER 2
Portrait of Fibonacci (c.1170 - c.1240) 17
Fibonacci: The Mathematical "Blockhead" 18
Activities:
    Fibonacci Discoveries 20
    Does 64 = 65? 21
    The Path From Pisa 22
    Fibonacci Magic 23
    More Fibonacci Magic 24
    Fibonacci's Golden Ratios 25
    On The Road To Rome 26

CHAPTER 3
Portrait of Descartes (1596 - 1650) 27
René Descartes: Father of Analytic Geometry 28
Activities:
    Plot and Swat 30
    On A Roll: A Game for Two Players 31
    Area The Easy Way 32
    Descartes' Word Search 33
    The Best Put to Test: A Skit to Read 34

CHAPTER 4
Portrait of Agnesi (1718 - 1799) 37
Maria Agnesi: The Sleeping Problem Solver 38
Activities:
    The Witch of Agnesi 41
    Exploring Isoperimetric Figures 42
    X's, Y's, and Zzzzz's: A Skit to Read 43
    Maria's Puzzle 45

CHAPTER 5
Portrait of Lagrange (1736 - 1813) 47
Joseph L. Lagrange: Making Measurement Metric 48
Activities:
    Lagrange's Four Square Theorem 50
    Predictable Products 51
    The Metric Highway 52
    Metric Crossword 53
    Metric Mania 54

CHAPTER 6
Portrait of Somerville (1780 - 1872) 55
Mary Somerville: The Queen of 19th Century Science 56
Activities:
    Just Passing Through 58
    Star Shapes 59
    Where Does The Ocean End? 60
    An Ant Thermometer 61

CHAPTER 7
Portrait of Dodgson (1832 - 1898) 63
Charles Dodgson: Mathematician in Wonderland 64
Activities:
    Dodgson's Doublets 66
    Dodgson's Discovery 67
    Lighthearted Logic 68
    More Logic Puzzles 69
    The Real Alice: A Skit to Read 70

CHAPTER 8
Portrait of Venn (1834 - 1923) 73
John Venn: Diagram Designer 74
Activities:
    Problem Solving Using Venn Diagrams 76
    Venn Diagrams Solve the Problem 77
    Who's in Charge? 78
    Crossing the River 79
    Rowing Relays 80

CHAPTER 9
Portrait of Noether (1882 - 1935) 81
Emmy Noether: Changing The Face of Algebra 82
Activities:
    A New Kind of Arithmetic 84
    Algebra Magic 85
    Algebra Solves the Mystery: A Card Trick 86
A Puzzling Mystery 87

HISTORICAL CONNECTIONS IN MATHEMATICS
Volume III

*Resources for Using
History of Mathematics
in the Classroom*

Wilbert Reimer
Fresno Pacific University

Luetta Reimer
Fresno Pacific University

Brenda Wood, Illustrator
Leticia Rivera, Desktop Publisher

AIMS Education Foundation
Fresno, California

HISTORICAL CONNECTIONS IN MATHEMATICS
Volume III

This book contains materials developed by the AIMS Education Foundation. **AIMS** (**A**ctivities **I**ntegrating **M**athematics and **S**cience) began in 1981 with a grant from the National Science Foundation. The non-profit AIMS Education Foundation publishes hands-on instructional materials that build conceptual understanding. The foundation also sponsors a national program of professional development through which educators may gain expertise in teaching math and science.

Copyright © 1995, 2005, 2010 by the AIMS Education Foundation

All rights reserved. No part of this book or associated digital media may be reproduced or transmitted in any form or by any means—including photocopying, taping, or information storage/retrieval systems—except as noted below.

- A person or school purchasing this AIMS publication is hereby granted permission to make up to 200 copies of any portion of it (or the files on the accompanying disc), provided these copies will be used for educational purposes and only at one school site. The files on the accompanying disc may not be altered by any means.

- Workshop or conference presenters may make one copy of any portion of a purchased activity for each participant, with a limit of five activities per workshop or conference session.

- All copies must bear the AIMS Education Foundation copyright information.

AIMS users may purchase unlimited duplication rights for making more than 200 copies, for use at more than one school site, or for use on the Internet. Contact us or visit the AIMS website for complete details.

AIMS Education Foundation
P.O. Box 8120, Fresno, CA 93747-8120 • 888.733.2467 • aimsedu.org

ISBN 978-1-60519-027-3

Printed in the United States of America

CHAPTER 10
Portrait of Polya (1887 - 1985) 89
George Polya: Father of Problem Solving 90
Activities:
- Pouring With Pails 92
- The Locker Problem 93
- Flea Flight 94
- Box It Up 95
- Building Blocks 96
- Knight Pairs on the Chessboard 97

APPENDIX
- Centimeter Dot Paper 100
- Table of Primes 101
- Some Programs for the TI-83 Graphic Calculator 102

SUGGESTIONS AND SOLUTIONS 104
RESOURCES FOR LIBRARY AND CLASSROOM 115

INTRODUCTION AND SUGGESTIONS FOR TEACHERS

"One can invent mathematics without knowing much history. One can use mathematics without knowing much, if any, of its history. But one cannot have a mature appreciation of mathematics without a substantial knowledge of its history."
—*Abe Schenitzer*

Our goal in this series is to provide a collection of resources to help teachers integrate the history of mathematics into their teaching. While mathematics history textbooks abound, there are not many sources that combine concise biographical information with activities to use in the classroom. We hope that the problem-solving experiences, the portraits, and the anecdotal stories will facilitate a broad, natural linkage of human elements and mathematical concepts.

The value of using history in teaching mathematics continues to gain recognition in the United States and throughout the world. Providing a personal and cultural context for mathematics helps students sense the larger meaning and scope of their studies. When they learn how persons have discovered and developed mathematics, they begin to understand that posing and solving problems is a distinctly human activity.

Using history in the mathematics classroom is often a successful motivational tool. Especially when combined with manipulatives, illustrations, and relevant applications, historical elements have the power to make mathematics "come alive" as never before. By viewing mathematics from a historical perspective, students learn that the *process* of problem solving is often as valuable as the *solution*.

This book can be used in many ways. The teacher may choose to read or share biographical information and anecdotes as an introduction to one or more of the activities in a particular section. Portraits may be posted or distributed, and puzzles or problems may be used independently. It may be most effective, however, to focus on one mathematician at a time. A wide range of activities may be incorporated into a unit on a specific mathematician, allowing the teacher to make cross-disciplinary connections with social studies, language arts, and science.

Mathematicians may be selected for emphasis according to the concepts being introduced in the mathematics curriculum, or they may be selected at random for enrichment. While some of the activities do not precisely replicate the problems the mathematicians worked on, they represent the areas of interest of those mathematicians. Activities have been chosen to appeal to a wide range of interests and ability levels.

A unique feature of this volume is the collection of programs for the TI-83 calculator in the appendix. These make it easy to add a technological dimension to the problem solving in the activities. The programs may be modified for use with other programmable calculators.

Complete solutions for all the activities and specific suggestions for use are included in the back of this book.

Wilbert Reimer
Luetta Reimer

SOME GENERAL SUGGESTIONS ON HOW TO INTEGRATE MATHEMATICS HISTORY INTO THE CLASSROOM

Through reading aloud:

Students respond very positively to simply hearing stories read aloud. Build a collection of brief and interesting stories to read in the classroom. The two volumes of *Mathematicians Are People, Too* were written with this purpose in mind, but there are other sources as well. Enlarge and photocopy the illustrations in *Historical Connections in Mathematics* onto transparencies, displaying them at appropriate times during the reading.

Through writing:

Many options for writing projects arise from mathematics history. Students may research the life of a particular mathematician and write a report. They may read a biography or a historical novel about a mathematician and write a book review. They may be asked to write an imaginary interview, a newspaper story, a screenplay, or a poem about an individual from mathematics history.

Other possibilities include writing about the origin of a particular concept or symbol, such as the = sign or ϖ. Some might wish to write about how mathematics was understood in a particular period or a particular place.

Through skits or video productions:

Choose a mathematician for special focus. Read to the class a brief biographical sketch or a collection of anecdotes about the mathematician being studied. We suggest the information in *Mathematicians Are People, Too, Volumes I and II*, or *Historical Connections in Mathematics, Volumes I, II, and III*. Older children may read and research on their own. Invite small groups of students to prepare a skit. If equipment is available, allow them to produce a video tape to share with the class.

Through hands-on experiences:

Some of the activities in this book invite hands-on experiences. While they may be done using paper and pencil, students will become more involved and remember the concepts better if they can participate more fully in the process. Encourage them to build models and to conduct experiments. Reinforce the principles of the scientific method as a problem-solving tool.

Through the arts:

Challenge students to draw or paint a scene from the life of the mathematician being studied. Remind them of the importance of researching the architecture, clothing, furnishings, etc. of the time and place in which the mathematician lived.

Ask students to write lyrics to a song or a poetic ballad that incorporates the major life events/accomplishments of a particular mathematician.

Through visual aids:

Consider displaying time lines, posters, portraits, or quotations from famous mathematicians. Check out the options in films and videos. Build a collection of postage stamps from various countries that honor mathematicians and mathematical development. Bake a cake and celebrate a mathematician's birthday!

Eratosthenes
c. 276 - c. 195 B.C.

ERATOSTHENES
THE EARTH MEASURER

Biographical Facts:

Eratosthenes (air-uh-TAHS-thuh-neez) was a Greek mathematician, geographer, and librarian. He was born in Cyrene, a Greek colony just west of Egypt, and lived from about 276 to 195 B.C.

Contributions:

Eratosthenes is best known for accurately calculating the circumference of the Earth. He also developed a mathematical procedure, known as "Eratosthenes' sieve," for finding prime numbers. At the University of Alexandria, he provided invaluable leadership as the chief librarian.

Anecdotes:

A Champ or Second Best?

Eratosthenes was an unusually well-rounded scholar. He read widely and wrote prolifically in philosophy, history, poetry, geography, astronomy, and mathematics. He studied at Plato's school in Athens and was admired by Archimedes.

Eratosthenes' friends gave him the nickname "Pentathlus"—a champion in five athletic events—in honor of his diversity. Others sometimes called him "Beta," meaning second. This may have insinuated that, while he was good at many things, he was only second-rate in most. More complimentary historians believe the nickname may have originated from the number that marked the door of Eratosthenes' lecture room or office.

The Great Librarian

Eratosthenes spent most of his life as chief librarian at the great University of Alexandria. The university was the first of its kind, and became a model for many universities today. It was efficiently designed with lecture rooms, laboratories, gardens, museums, and living quarters. At its core was an excellent library. About 40 years after its founding, the library held the largest collection of learned works in the world—over 600,000 papyrus rolls. Largely because of the university, Alexandria became and remained, for nearly 1000 years, the intellectual center of the Roman world.

Reading is Living

Eratosthenes lost his eyesight in old age. According to legend, the great scholar refused to eat. He would rather die, he said, than live without being able to read.

Measuring the Earth

Eratosthenes determined the circumference of the Earth by using an extremely simple and ingenious method. His procedure involved two locations: Syene, an Egyptian city on the Nile, and Alexandria, about 500 miles north. These two cities were thought to be on the same meridian. An imaginary line drawn through the north and south poles would pass through both cities.

At noon on the first day of summer, people in Syene had noticed that the sun cast no shadows. Eratosthenes confirmed this by observing water in deep wells; the bottom of these wells was completely illuminated by the sun's rays. There were no shadows on the water's surface from the sides of the well.

So Eratosthenes chose the first day of summer to put his plan into action. He identified a pillar in Alexandria and measured the angle of the pillar's shadow at high noon. He knew from geometry that if lines through the pillar in Alexandria and through a well in Syene could be extended to meet at the center of the Earth, the two lines would form an angle equal to that of the pillar's shadow. The geometric theorem states: "Parallel lines cut by a transversal form congruent alternate interior angles."

The angle made by the shadow on the pillar was approximately 7.5° (about 1/50th of an entire circle). Multiplying 50 times the distance from pillar to well (500 miles), Eratosthenes came very close to the Earth's circumference of about 25,000 miles.

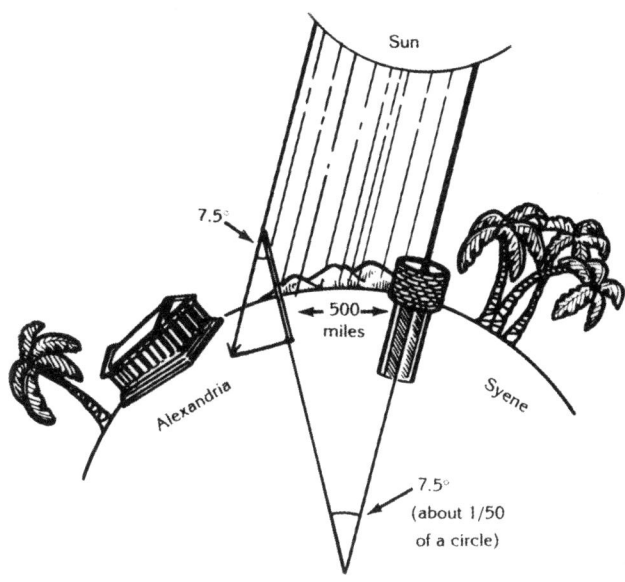

It is amazing that the size of the Earth could be determined so simply and so accurately without a telescope and without traveling great distances. Eratosthenes had demonstrated the incredible power of reason! (And he also showed that he knew the Earth was round, long before Columbus!)

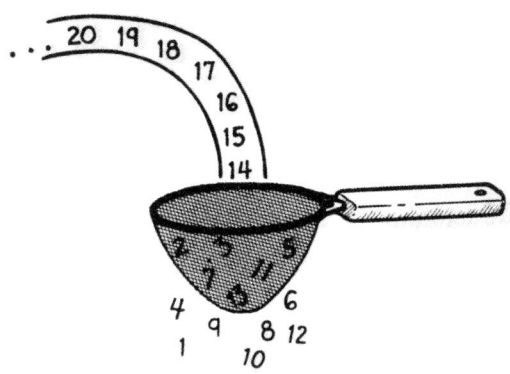

The Sieve of Eratosthenes

Prime numbers have intrigued people for thousands of years. A *prime number* is a counting number that has exactly two divisors. The Latin word *primus* means first in importance. The primes lead to important properties of numbers. Counting numbers that have *more* than two divisors are called *composite numbers*.

Various methods have been developed for finding prime numbers. Among Eratosthenes' most important contributions is his famous "sieve," a simple technique that eliminates composite numbers, leaving primes "caught" in the sieve of Eratosthenes.

THE SIEVE OF ERATOSTHENES
A METHOD FOR FINDING PRIMES

1	2	3	4	5	6	7	8	9	10
11	12	13	14	15	16	17	18	19	20
21	22	23	24	25	26	27	28	29	30
31	32	33	34	35	36	37	38	39	40
41	42	43	44	45	46	47	48	49	50
51	52	53	54	55	56	57	58	59	60
61	62	63	64	65	66	67	68	69	70
71	72	73	74	75	76	77	78	79	80
81	82	83	84	85	86	87	88	89	90
91	92	93	94	95	96	97	98	99	100

Follow the instructions to find all the prime numbers between 1 and 100 using the method developed by Eratosthenes.

INSTRUCTIONS

Cross out 1, since it is not classified as a prime number.

Draw a circle around 2, the smallest prime number. Then cross out every second number after 2.

Draw a circle around 3, the next prime number. Then cross out every third number after 3. Some numbers will be crossed out more than once.

Circle the next open number, 5. Then cross out every fifth number after 5.

The next open number is 7. Circle 7 and then cross out every seventh number after 7.

Go through the grid and draw a circle around every number that has not yet been crossed out. The circled numbers are all the prime numbers between 1 and 100.

You should have found a total of 25 primes between 1 and 100.

PRIME MAGIC

Find prime numbers to put in the empty spaces to complete the magic squares. Make sure each number you use is a prime by using Eratosthenes' sieve or a table of primes. Remember, in a magic square the sum of the numbers in each row, column, and diagonal must be the same.

Hint: The "magic" total for each row, column, and diagonal is always three times the number in the center square.

47		101
	59	

157		43
	127	

	7	
	73	
		37

277		
	157	
151		

107		29
	89	

	71	
41		59

HISTORICAL CONNECTIONS VOL. III   © 2010 AIMS Education Foundation

IS IT ALWAYS TRUE?

Eratosthenes designed a simple way for finding prime numbers when he made his famous "sieve." Since Eratosthenes' work more than 2000 years ago, mathematicians have been fascinated with the properties of prime numbers.

In 1742, a German mathematician named Goldbach conjectured (guessed or surmised) that every even number except two is the sum of two primes. Although many brilliant persons have studied this problem, the conjecture has never been proven or disproven.

Verify Goldbach's conjecture for these even numbers by expressing each of them as the sum of two primes.

1. 6 = ☐ + ☐
2. 10 = ☐ + ☐
3. 14 = ☐ + ☐
4. 18 = ☐ + ☐
5. 22 = ☐ + ☐
6. 24 = ☐ + ☐
7. 28 = ☐ + ☐
8. 40 = ☐ + ☐
9. 64 = ☐ + ☐
10. 100 = ☐ + ☐

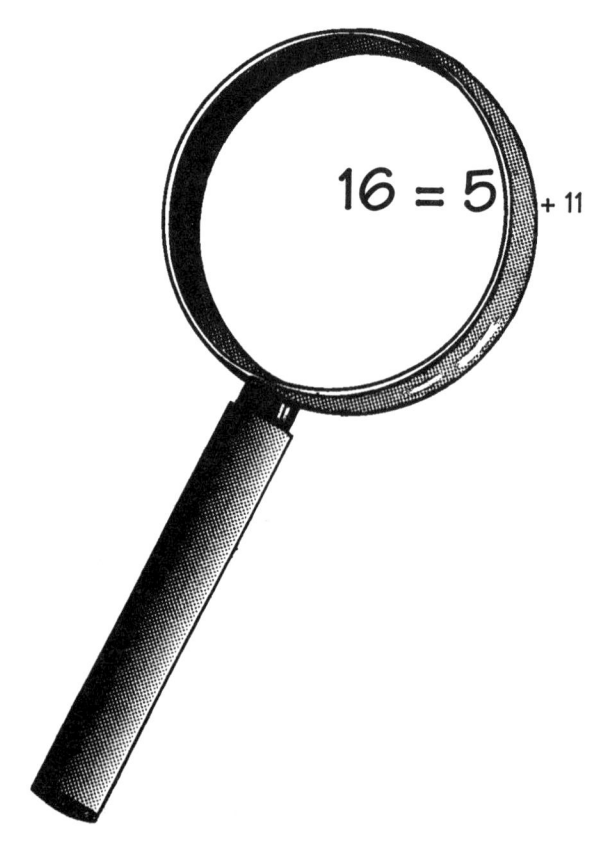

16 = 5 + 11

HISTORICAL CONNECTIONS VOL. III © 2010 AIMS EDUCATION FOUNDATION

ODDS IN THE MAKING

After Eratosthenes (in about 200 B. C.) discovered a way to find prime numbers, many other mathematicians looked for interesting properties about primes.

One conjecture was that every odd number is the sum of a prime and a power of 2.

For example, $25 = 17 + 2^3$ or $17 + 8$.

Show that the conjecture stated above is true for the odd numbers shown in the table on the right.

Remember, prime numbers are
    2, 3, 5, 7, 11, 13, 17, 19, 23, 29, 31, 37, 41, 43, 47, 53, etc.

and the powers of 2 are
    1, 2, 4, 8, 16, 32, 64, 128, 256, etc.

Don't be surprised if there is more than one solution.

Odd Number	Prime	Power of Two
9	5	4
11	7	4
13	11	2
15		
17		
19		
21		
23		
25		
27		
49		
67		
89		
119		
131		

HISTORICAL CONNECTIONS VOL. III   © 2010 AIMS Education Foundation

THE EARTH AND THE WIRE BELT

In about 200 B.C., Eratosthenes found a method for successfully measuring the Earth's circumference. He was the first person to discover that the circumference was about 25,000 miles.

Suppose the Earth had a wire belt tightly wrapped around it at the equator. The length of this belt would be approximately 25,000 miles.

Now, suppose we cut this belt and inserted an extra piece of wire 100 feet long.

If the belt were raised equidistantly all around the Earth, how high above the ground would the belt be?

Most people guess a fraction of an inch. The correct answer is surprising. **Almost sixteen feet!**

This is easily proven using some simple algebra and geometry.

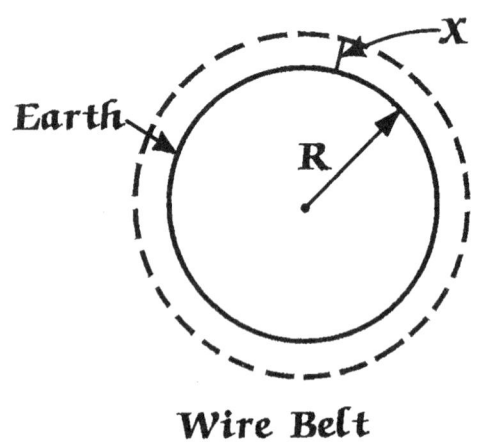

Let x represent the distance the wire belt is raised equidistantly above the Earth.

Then, $2\pi R + 100 = 2\pi(R + x)$, or
$2\pi R + 100 = 2\pi R + 2\pi x$.

Solving this equation for x gives
$$x = \frac{100}{2\pi}, \text{ or}$$

$$x = 15.9 \text{ feet!}$$

How does the radius of the Earth affect the answer to this problem?

Fibonacci
c. 1170 - c. 1240

FIBONACCI
THE MATHEMATICAL "BLOCKHEAD"

Biographical Facts:

Fibonacci (fee-boh-NAH-chee) was the nickname Leonardo of Pisa gave himself. He lived in Italy from about 1170 to 1240. The son of a wealthy customs official, Fibonacci traveled widely, especially in Arabic countries, absorbing the mathematical knowledge of the Islamic world.

Contributions:

Fibonacci was one of the earliest Europeans to write about algebra. His most important book, *Liber abaci*, promoted the use of Hindu-Arabic numerals in Europe. He also worked in number theory, and introduced the number sequence that bears his name, the Fibonacci sequence. Fibonacci was the first to write fractions with a bar to separate the denominator and numerator.

Anecdotes:

The Leaning Tower

In 12th century Italy, the little town of Pisa bustled with excitement. The beautiful cathedral started more than 100 years earlier was finally completed, and construction had begun on the nearby eight-story bell tower. But after the first three stories were built, the engineer and his workmen noticed that the foundation was settling unevenly. Extra height was added to the short side, but the additional weight just made the foundation sink more. Two centuries later, when the tower was finished, it was still leaning. And so it leans today, much to the delight of tourists from all around the world.

The Privilege of School

One of the youths who watched the early stages of the tower construction was a boy named Leonard, whose father, Bonacci, was a well-to-do businessman and government official. Leonard was a bright student who worked hard at his studies. He knew it was a privilege to go to school, though students today would probably not consider sitting cross-legged on the floor a privilege! Leonard and his classmates learned primarily through oral lecturing, and were expected to memorize the material they recorded with bone styluses on wax tablets. The styluses were pointed on one end for writing, and blunt on the other for erasing.

The students studied grammar and logic, as well as geometry, astronomy, music, and arithmetic. Most of the arithmetic consisted of word problems, more like riddles than problems that might lead to mathematical principles. All of the computation was done using Roman numerals. Adding and subtracting them was not too difficult, but to multiply and divide, everyone in Pisa relied on the abacus.

A First Glimpse at Numbers

When his father was sent to Bougie, Algeria, to serve as customs official in a Pisan warehouse, Fibonacci went along. These travels were the most important influence on his later work. He visited Constantinople, Egypt, Syria, Sicily, and Provence. He marveled at the ease with which the Mediterranean merchants kept their accounts; they were using Hindu-Arabic numerals instead of Roman numerals.

In 1202, Fibonacci published his great life work, *Liber Abaci* ("Book of the Abacus"), in which he introduced and explained the Hindu-Arabic numeral system. The book began:

> The nine Indian figures are:
> 1, 2, 3, 4, 5, 6, 7, 8, 9.
> With these nine figures, and with the sign 0, any number may be written.

Fibonacci carefully demonstrated the Hindu-Arabic methods of calculation through a series of problems, and convincingly showed their superiority over the Roman numerals. His book ultimately revolutionized European mathematics by promoting the use of these numerals.

Listen to a Blockhead?
Not everyone was instantly persuaded by Fibonacci. There were plenty of skeptics. These persons' scorn may have been incited by the fact that Fibonacci sometimes signed his name "Leonardo Bigollo." The word "Bigollo" has more than one meaning; it may mean "traveler," which Fibonacci certainly was, but it also means "blockhead." Fibonacci felt that many of his contemporaries considered him a "blockhead" for expressing so much interest in the Hindu-Arabic numerals. One story says he delighted in using this signature to show the European world what a "blockhead" could do. Today, Fibonacci is considered the greatest mathematician of the middle ages.

The Fibonacci Numbers
Fibonacci is probably best known for a famous sequence of numbers: 1, 1, 2, 3, 5, 8, 13, 21, 34, 55, 89, 144,… Each term in the sequence is obtained by adding the two previous terms. Fibonacci introduced this sequence in conjunction with a problem dealing with the offspring of rabbits. The numbers in the sequence can quickly provide the total number of rabbits in a population after any number of generations.

In the 1870s, centuries after Fibonacci's findings, many examples of the Fibonacci sequence were discovered in nature. Botanists found that the patterns of leaf buds on some stems followed the Fibonacci sequence. The spirals of seeds in the head of a sunflower display these numbers, as do the petals on artichokes and the scales on pineapples.

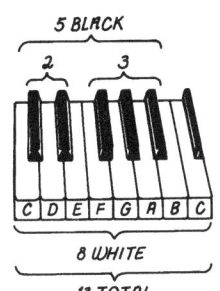

Fibonacci numbers can also be observed on the keyboard of a piano: an octave is made up of 5 black keys (in groups of 2 and 3) and 8 white keys, for a total of 13. All of these numbers are Fibonacci numbers.

The sequence also contains many fascinating number relationships and patterns. For example, the sum of the squares of any two consecutive Fibonacci numbers is always another Fibonacci number. And, the sum of any ten consecutive Fibonacci numbers is always evenly divisible by 11. These are only two examples of the almost unlimited mathematical properties available for discovery in the sequence.

The Golden Rectangle
The golden rectangle is the most popular rectangular shape in art and architecture as well as in daily living. Studies have shown that people from many cultures prefer it to rectangles of other proportions. In a golden rectangle, the ratio of the shorter side to the longer side is approximately 0.618. This number is approximated by dividing any Fibonacci number by the next number in the sequence.

The golden rectangle's power may be observed in masterpieces like the great Egyptian pyramids and the Parthenon in Athens and in everyday objects like 3-by-5 cards and light switch plates.

FIBONACCI DISCOVERIES

1, 1, 2, 3, 5, 8, 13, 21, 34, 55, 89, 144

Fibonacci Challenge No. 1

The above sequence of numbers is called the Fibonacci sequence. Do you see a pattern? Find the next three numbers in the sequence.

1, 1, 2, 3, 5, 8, 13, 21, 34, 55, 89, 144, ____, ____, ____,

Fibonacci Challenge No. 2

Take any Fibonacci number and square it. Next, find the product of the Fibonacci numbers preceding and following the number squared. Compare this product with the square of the number. Complete the table below to find a pattern.

Fibonacci Number	2	3	5	8	13	21	34	55
Square of Number				64				
Product of Numbers Before and After				65				
Difference								

Fibonacci Challenge No. 3

Observe the pattern which occurs when the squares of Fibonacci numbers are added. Use your discovery to complete the illustration.

$1^2 = 1 \times 1$
$1^2 + 1^2 = 1 \times 2$
$1^2 + 1^2 + 2^2 = 2 \times 3$
$1^2 + 1^2 + 2^2 + 3^2 = 3 \times 5$
$1^2 + 1^2 + 2^2 + 3^2 + 5^2 = $ ___ x ___
$1^2 + 1^2 + 2^2 + 3^2 + 5^2 + 8^2 = $ ___ x ___
$1^2 + 1^2 + 2^2 + 3^2 + 5^2 + 8^2 + 13^2 = $ ___ x ___

HISTORICAL CONNECTIONS VOL. III © 2010 AIMS EDUCATION FOUNDATION

DOES 64 = 65?

Cut this 8 by 8 square (which has an area of 64 square units) into four pieces as marked.

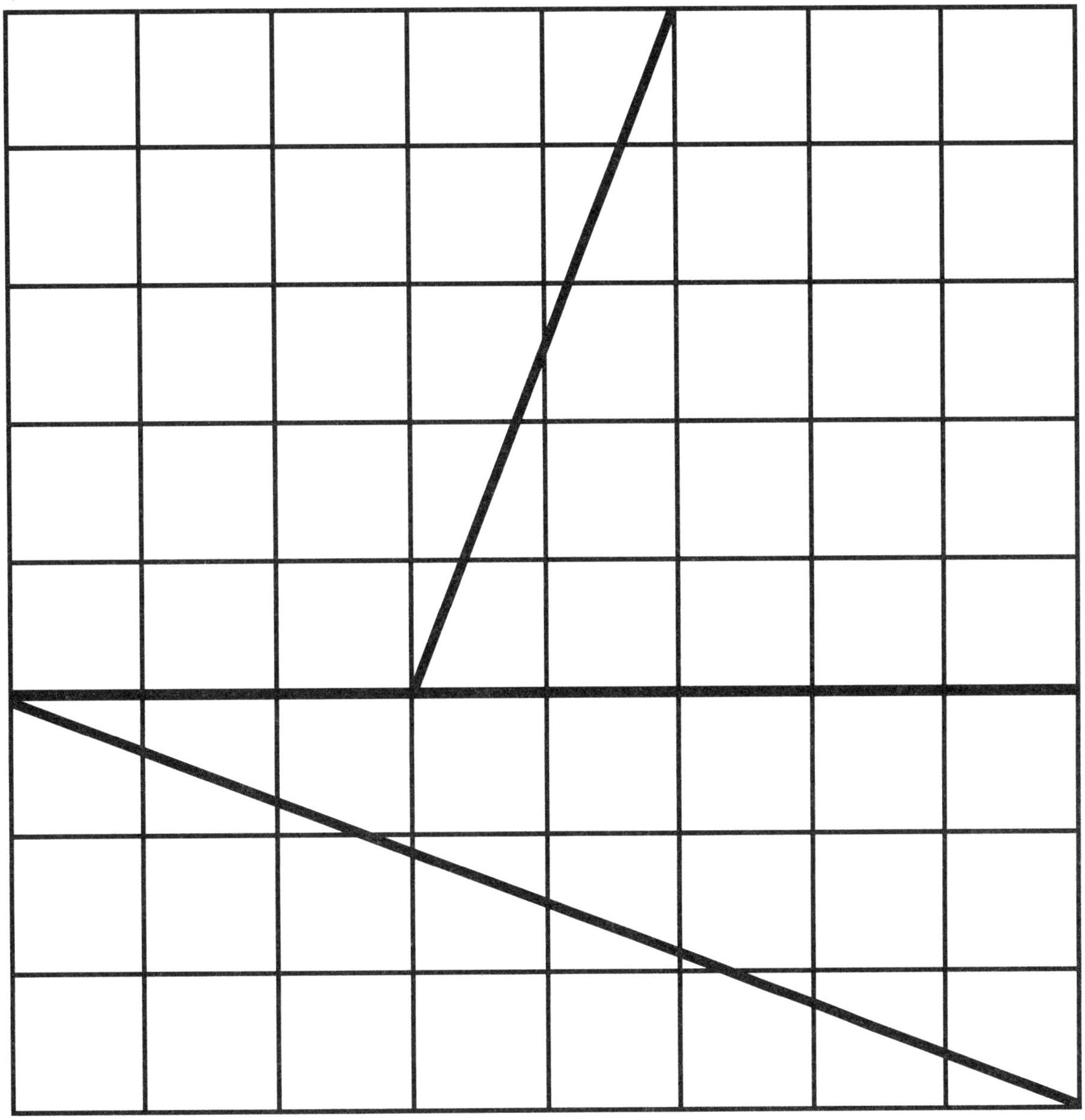

Now, form a rectangle as shown in this diagram. What is the area of the rectangle? Does this mean that 64 = 65? Can you explain this?

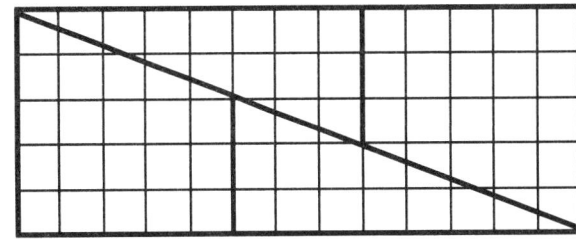

Make other shapes with the four pieces and determine their areas. You may wish to record the shapes and areas on graph paper.

HISTORICAL CONNECTIONS VOL. III © 2010 AIMS EDUCATION FOUNDATION

THE PATH FROM PISA

Suppose a craftsman is designing a short path in honor of Leonard of Pisa, also known as Fibonacci. He has ten 1 by 2 tiles with which to cover a 2 by 10 rectangular path. In how many different ways can these ten tiles be arranged?

Solve this problem by first arranging tiles on a 2 by 1 rectangle, then a 2 by 2, and so on until you discover the pattern that emerges. Record your results in the table.

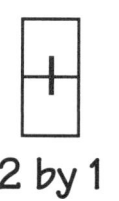

2 by 1

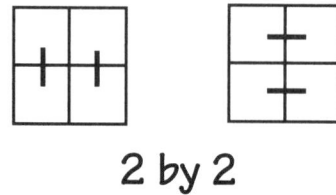

2 by 2

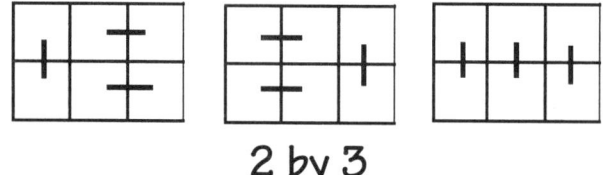

2 by 3

Dimensions	Number of Arrangements
2 by 1	1
2 by 2	2
2 by 3	3
2 by 4	_____ (not 4)
2 by 5	_____
2 by 6	_____
2 by 7	_____
2 by 8	_____
2 by 9	_____
2 by 10	_____

What famous number sequence does the pattern in the table resemble?

HISTORICAL CONNECTIONS VOL. III © 2010 AIMS Education Foundation

FIBONACCI MAGIC

The famous Fibonacci sequence begins 1, 1, 2, 3, 5, 8, 13, . . . Each term is the sum of the previous two terms.

Create a *Fibonacci-like* sequence by starting with *any* two numbers. Extend the sequence by repeatedly adding the two previous terms. Here are some examples:

>4, 7, 11, 18, 29, 47, 76, ...
>
>2, 5, 7, 12, 19, 31, 50, 81, 131, ...
>
>1, 6, 7, 13, 20, 33, 53, 86, ...

Here's a magic trick to perform with any Fibonacci-like sequence.

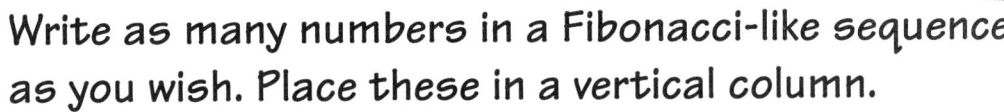

Write as many numbers in a Fibonacci-like sequence as you wish. Place these in a vertical column.

Draw a line between any two numbers listed.

Secret: the sum of the numbers *above the line* will always be the second number below the line minus the second number from the beginning!

Here's an example:

```
  2
  4
  6
 10
 16
 26
 42
———
 68
110
```

Subtract 4 from 110 to get 106, the sum of the numbers above the line!

Make up some sequences of your own and try this trick with your friends!

This works every time, regardless of the numbers you use to begin your Fibonacci-like sequence. Can you discover why?

MORE FIBONACCI MAGIC

Build a *Fibonacci-like* sequence by choosing any two numbers. Extend the sequence by adding the two previous terms. Here are some examples:

4, 7, 11, 18, 29, 47, 76, …

2, 5, 7, 12, 19, 31, 50, 81, 131, …

1, 6, 7, 13, 20, 33, 53, 86, …

Try this magic trick with your friends:

1. Have someone write down the first ten terms of any Fibonacci-like sequence.
2. After your friend has written down the seventh term, announce that you already know what the sum of the first ten terms will be! (Secretly write this sum on a sheet of paper.)
3. Ask your friend to continue building the sequence until ten terms have been listed. Then instruct your friend to find the sum of the first ten terms.

It should be the same as what you wrote down earlier! Show your paper to prove it!

Secret: the sum of ten terms in a Fibonacci-like sequence is always 11 times the seventh term.

Can you show why this will always work?

FIBONACCI'S GOLDEN RATIOS

1, 1, 2, 3, 5, 8, 13, 21, 34, 55, 89, 144

A Fibonacci ratio is defined as a ratio formed by two consecutive Fibonacci numbers. $\frac{2}{3}$ $\frac{5}{8}$ $\frac{13}{21}$ are examples of Fibonacci ratios.

Complete this table to help you discover an amazing fact about Fibonacci ratios. You may wish to use a calculator.

Fibonacci Ratio	Expressed to Three Decimal Places
$\frac{1}{1}$	
$\frac{1}{2}$	
$\frac{2}{3}$	
$\frac{3}{5}$	
$\frac{5}{8}$	
$\frac{8}{13}$	
$\frac{13}{21}$	
$\frac{21}{34}$	
$\frac{34}{55}$	
$\frac{55}{89}$	

What unusual number do the Fibonacci ratios appear to be approaching? In mathematics this is an important number known as the Golden Ratio. The ratio is considered especially pleasing by artists and architects, and may be found in many of the world's great masterpieces.

Try forming these ratios for *Fibonacci-like* sequences. What is amazing about the result?

HISTORICAL CONNECTIONS VOL. III © 2010 AIMS EDUCATION FOUNDATION

ON THE ROAD TO ROME

Fibonacci was a great Italian mathematician who lived in the 13th century. He loved brainteasers. This puzzle comes from his most important book, *Liber abaci*.

There are seven old women on the road to Rome.
Each woman has seven mules;
each mule carries seven sacks;
each sack contains seven loaves;
with each loaf are seven knives;
and each knife is in seven sheaths.
Women, mules, sacks, loaves, knives, and sheaths, how many are there in all on the road to Rome?

Can you solve this Fibonacci puzzle?

Descartes
1596 - 1650

RENÉ DESCARTES
FATHER OF ANALYTIC GEOMETRY

Biographical Facts:

René Descartes (day-KART) was born in La Haye, Touraine, about 200 miles south of Paris, on March 31, 1596. Descartes' mother died a few days after his birth. His father, Joachim Descartes, a Councillor of the Parliament, used his good position to provide excellent care for his young son. Never physically robust, Descartes died of pneumonia in Sweden after moving there in 1650 to tutor Queen Christina.

Contributions:

Descartes may be best known as a philosopher, but his contribution to mathematics dramatically shaped mathematical thought. His short book, *Geometry*, was published as an appendix in 1637. Descartes showed the power of combining algebra and geometry. This revolutionized the applicability of algebra and led to the development of analytic geometry, also named Cartesian geometry in Descartes' honor. Descartes originated much of the exponential notation used today. He standardized the use of the first letters of the alphabet to denote known quantities and the use of the last letters of the alphabet to denote unknown quantities.

Quotations by Descartes:

"Perfect numbers like perfect men are very rare."

"I hope that posterity will judge me kindly not only as to the things which I have explained, but also to those which I have intentionally omitted so as to leave to others the pleasure of discovery."

"Mathematics is a more powerful instrument of knowledge than any other that has been bequeathed to us by human agency."

"I think, therefore I am."

"The reading of all good books is like a conversation with the finest people of past centuries."

Anecdotes:

The Sleepy Head

When Descartes was eight years old, his father enrolled him in the Jesuit College at La Fleche. It was an excellent school; Descartes spent five years studying grammar and literature, and another three years studying science, philosophy, and theology. His favorite subject was mathematics.

When Descartes arrived at the school, the director, Father Charlet, noticed how frail and weak Descartes was. Charlet became fond of the boy and to build up Descartes' body, permitted him to stay in bed as long as he wished every morning. This became a lifelong habit for Descartes, who claimed that these hours of lying in bed were his most productive thinking periods—the source of all his great ideas in philosophy and mathematics.

The Fly's the Hero!

Once, when Descartes was resting in his bed, he noticed a fly crawling around on the ceiling. As the fly meandered near the corner, Descartes thought of how he could

HISTORICAL CONNECTIONS VOL. III © 2010 AIMS EDUCATION FOUNDATION

mathematically describe the fly's position. Suddenly, he realized that he could express the fly's position in terms of its distance from the adjacent walls. This was the birth of Descartes' great contribution to mathematics—coordinate geometry, recognized today as the basis of all modern applied mathematics.

Descartes' Dreams

Descartes had three dreams in one night that changed his life. It was November 10, 1619. He said the dreams clarified his purpose in life and determined his future by revealing "a marvelous science" and "a wonderful discovery." No one knows exactly what Descartes saw, but afterwards Descartes was convinced that mathematics was the key to the secrets of nature. All of the sciences, he believed, were interconnected by mathematical links. The dreams showed Descartes that "…the entire universe is a great, harmonious, and mathematically designed machine."

A Dapper Gentleman

Descartes enjoyed dressing to make an impression. For an evening out on the town, he wore a fashionable taffeta coat, buckled on his shining sword, and topped it off with a sweeping, broad-brimmed, ostrich-plumed hat. Descartes' manner was just as gallant. Once, when the lady he was escorting was assaulted by a drunk on the street, Descartes whipped out his sword, flicked the weapon out of the attacker's hand, and pinned him to the ground. He would have killed him, he explained later, but the man was too dirty to be butchered in front of a beautiful lady.

Study Those Languages!

In 1621, Descartes booked passage on a boat headed for Frisia. When the crew noticed his fancy clothes and elegant style, they plotted to knock him out, rob him, and throw him overboard. They made all these plans in front of Descartes, assuming he did not know their language. But Descartes understood every word. Before they had a chance to act, he whipped out his sword and ordered them to return him immediately to shore.

Summoned by a Queen

Descartes was comfortably living and working in Holland when he received an unusual invitation from Queen Christina of Sweden. She wanted Descartes to tutor her in philosophy. She hoped Descartes would help her plan a top-notch academy of sciences for Sweden.

Descartes was not eager to go. He dreaded the cold weather, and had heard stories of the whimsical, tomboy queen. But 19-year-old Christina insisted. She sent one of her admirals to Holland to persuade Descartes.

Although Descartes was widely honored upon his arrival in Sweden, his worst fears came true. Christina wanted her lessons every morning at 5:00 o'clock in the unheated library with the windows wide open. She was indifferent to heat and cold, and she only slept five hours a night. But Descartes was used to staying in bed until noon, and could not take the cold. Soon he caught pneumonia and on February 11, 1650, died at the age of 54.

Moving the Bones

Descartes, who never married, was buried in a small Catholic cemetery near the Queen's estate. Seventeen years later, his remains were moved to Paris and re-entombed in what is now the Pantheon. Most of them were, that is. The French treasurer-general, who supervised the move of the body, kept the bones from Descartes' right hand as a personal souvenir. About this, the great mathematician Jacobi said, "It is often more convenient to possess the ashes of great men than to possess the men themselves during their lifetime."

PLOT AND SWAT

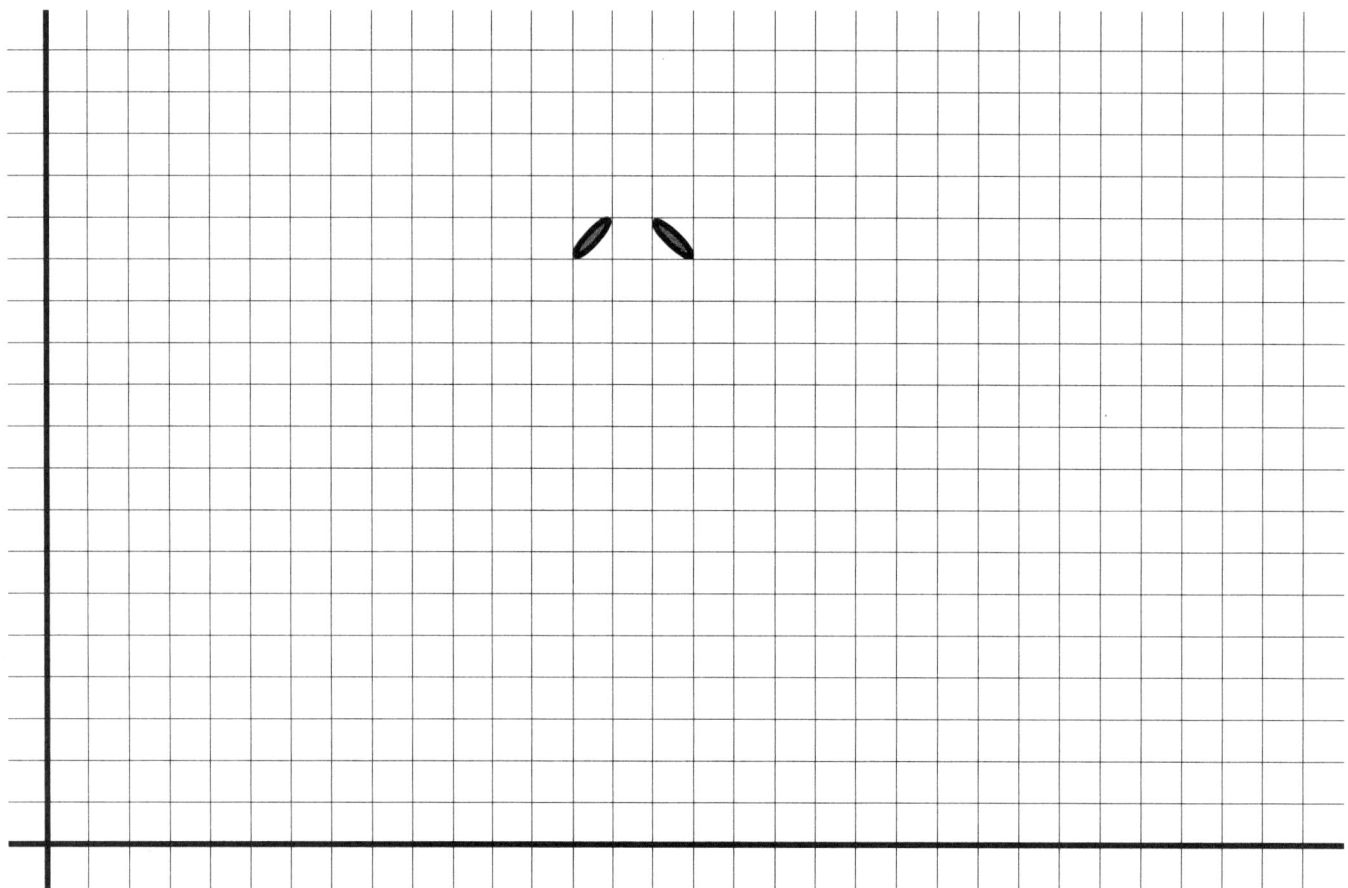

Plot and connect the following points to see what Descartes saw on his ceiling.

a. (9,18) (11, 16) (10,14) (13,11)
b. (16,11) (21,13) (24,13) (28,11) (26,9) (22,8) (18,8) (16,8) (16,5) (15,3) (14,3)
c. (11,8) (10,6) (8,4)
d. (16,8) (18,5) (17,3) (19,1)
e. (13,11) (13,14) (14,15) (15,15) (16,14) (16,11)
f. (21,4) (19,6) (18,8)
g. (20,18) (18,16) (19,14) (16,11)
h. (13,8) (11,8) (7,8) (3,9) (1,11) (5,13) (8,13) (13,11)
i. (10,1) (12,3) (11,5) (13,8) (13,5) (14,3)

ON A ROLL
A Game for Two Players

```
6  .  .  .  .  .  .
5  .  .  .  .  .  .
4  .  .  .  .  .  .
Red  3  .  .  .  .  .  .
2  .  .  .  .  .  .
1  .  .  .  .  .  .
   1  2  3  4  5  6
        White
```

Materials needed: Four dice, two white and two red (or other color); a grid of points like the one above. (Use dot paper or draw your own.)

Instructions for Playing:

1. Each player rolls one die. The player with the higher number goes first.

2. The first player tosses all four dice. After selecting one white and one red die, the player marks the point represented by the two numbers on the grid with an X.

3. The second player also tosses the dice and chooses a point based on the numbers on one white and one red die. This player circles the chosen point.

4. A point may be chosen only once.

5. The first player to get four X's or four circles in a vertical, horizontal, or diagonal row wins.

AREA THE EASY WAY

Thanks to Descartes and the creation of analytic geometry, many complex problems in mathematics have amazingly simple solutions. Consider, for example, the problem of finding the area of any polygon using the coordinates of the vertices.

Discover the easy way to solve this problem by observing the example below. This procedure will work for polygons of any shape or any number of vertices.

INSTRUCTIONS
1. Beginning with any vertex, list the coordinates of the vertices in order, moving counter-clockwise around the polygon. List the first pair again at the end.
2. Find the diagonal products from left to right.
3. Find the diagonal products from right to left.
4. Sum each column of products.
5. Find their difference and divide by 2.
This is the polygon's area!

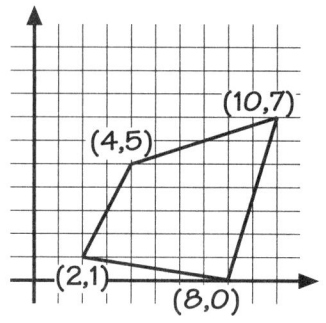

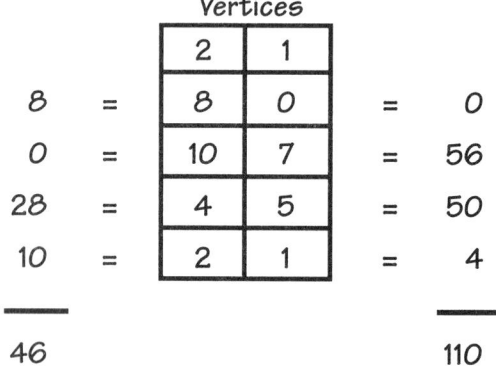

Find the area for each polygon using the above method.

(1) 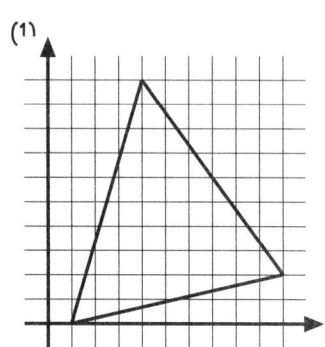   (2) 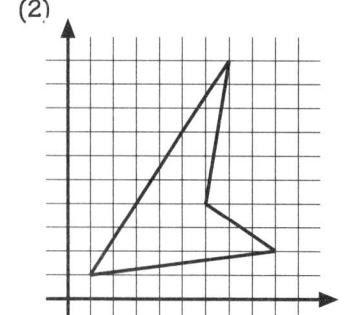   (3)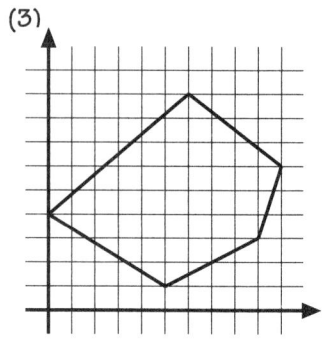

HISTORICAL CONNECTIONS VOL. III © 2010 AIMS Education Foundation

DESCARTES' WORD SEARCH

Circle the analytic geometry terms listed below. They may appear in the puzzle forward, backward, horizontally, vertically, or diagonally.

```
C N D P O I N T O U D A T Z N M
C I T K B S R G C W K P J O B I
K E R J C D E C N A T S I D Y E
C A E C A M I P O S I T I V E C
Y L M S L P N E G R A O F I D O
B G E O M E T R Y U I G C P Q J
H E M C G N A P Q I L G D R U E
U B F E A P F E O N H E I B A N
A R U N H T B N G R K Q G N D F
N A T A Z O R D I N A T E C R I
O E Z L F R N I O T N S I X A M
N X G P H U L C K I C O K E N P
A S M A F L X U Y R H T U R T M
M R H E T W A L O B A R A P P S
C O O R D I N A T E S P B G I Z
G R S L X U V R A B S C I S S A
S E T R A C S E D T W S P A E W
```

ABSCISSA	EQUATION	PERPENDICULAR
ALGEBRA	GEOMETRY	PLANE
AXIS	GRAPH	POINT
CIRCLE	NEGATIVE	POSITIVE
COORDINATES	ORDINATE	QUADRANT
DESCARTES	ORIGIN	
DISTANCE	PARABOLA	

THE BEST PUT TO TEST
A Skit to Read

Schoolmaster:	You look tired, Descartes.
Descartes:	I feel fine, sir.
Schoolmaster:	But your skin is so pale for a young boy. And you are much too thin. Are you eating enough at your meals?
Descartes:	Yes, sir. Perhaps I am just small for my age.
Schoolmaster:	No, I think something is wrong. You need more rest. From now on, you will stay in bed until noon. You may get up in time for lunch. Understood?
Descartes:	Yes, sir.
Narrator 1:	Descartes had always been a little weaker than other boys his age. He couldn't run as fast or play as hard as other children. But when the schoolmaster said he could stay in bed until noon, the other boys were jealous.
Henry:	Look at Descartes! He'll snore until the moon comes out.
George:	I can't believe the schoolmaster thinks that staying in bed will make him stronger!
Charles:	Yeah. He needs to get out in the sunshine. If he'd practice football with us, he'd have to be strong!
Henry:	(sneering) We'll see you later, sleepyhead.
George:	Some of us have to go to classes!
Narrator 2:	Descartes usually woke early in the morning. He found it funny that the boys thought he was sleeping when he was really only pretending. Sometimes he would snore extra loud, just to hear their reactions!
Narrator 3:	When the boys left for their classes, Descartes lay in bed and thought. Sometimes he memorized poetry. Other times, he worked on mathematics problems. Usually, he worked the problems in his head, without paper or pencil. He was never bored.
Narrator 1:	The schoolmaster's plan became a habit for Descartes. Throughout his life, he stayed in bed long after the sun had risen. It was in the comfort of his bed that his mathematical mind worked best. But one day, his leisurely mornings came to an end.
Messenger:	Sir, I have a message for you. It is a letter from Queen Christina of Sweden.
Descartes:	A letter from the queen of Sweden? What does it say?
Messenger:	Queen Christina invites you to come to Sweden to tutor her. She praises your ability and wants teaching from the best mathematician in the world—you.
Descartes:	Come to Sweden! She must be out of her mind. I'm retired here in Holland, and the climate agrees with me. Why should I leave my comfortable home

	and beautiful gardens for the bitter cold in Sweden? No, I will not tutor her. Please send her my regrets.
Narrator 2:	Weeks passed and Descartes forgot about the message. But Queen Christina did not.
Queen Christina:	What? He refuses to come! I cannot believe it! Perhaps he misunderstood. I want him in Sweden. We *need* him in Sweden. Send a delegation at once to persuade him to come. Bring him back with you on my ship.
Narrator 3:	When Descartes heard that Queen Christina was beginning a new school of science and mathematics, he reconsidered. Maybe he did have a responsibility to share his knowledge. He packed as many warm clothes as he could for the journey. It was winter in Sweden and bitterly cold.
Queen Christina:	Welcome, Descartes. I am pleased to see you changed your mind.
Descartes:	You gave me little choice, Your Highness.
Queen Christina:	Surely you do not blame me for wanting to learn from the best. You will see that Sweden is not such a bad place. We will begin our tutoring sessions tomorrow morning, at five o'clock.
Descartes:	In the morning? Your Highness, I am not used to getting up that early. Perhaps I would teach more effectively in the afternoon.
Queen Christina:	Descartes, I am a very busy queen. I cannot wait until the afternoon to learn mathematics. I have many other appointments. I will see you at 5:00 a.m. in the library.
Narrator 1:	With that, Queen Christina swooshed out of the room. Descartes stood numbed.
Descartes:	What have I gotten into? How can she do this to me? She is only a child—barely nineteen years old! She does not realize my limitations. However, she is the queen. Now that I'm here, it is my responsibility to obey.
Narrator 2:	Descartes got up every morning to tutor Queen Christina at five o'clock. It was dark and the cold wind stung his cheeks, but Descartes obeyed her wishes.
Descartes:	Queen Christina, I have been coming every day to teach you, and I am pleased with your progress. But I am not used to the cold Swedish winters. Would it be possible to close the library windows to keep out the draft?
Queen Christina:	Oh, my. Surely you know that cold temperatures are best for the brain! Just take a deep breath and enjoy the fresh air.
Narrator 3:	Descartes bundled up in as many clothes as he could, but he could not stay warm. After a short time in Sweden, he caught pneumonia and died.
Narrator 1:	Queen Christina was wrong about a lot of things. But at least one time she was right! That was when she said that Descartes was one of the greatest and most influential mathematicians of all time.

Agnesi
1718 - 1799

MARIA AGNESI
THE SLEEPING PROBLEM SOLVER

Biographical Facts:

Maria Gaetana Agnesi (ah-NYA-zi) was an Italian mathematician born in Milan on May 16, 1718. Her parents were wealthy and well-educated. After studying and writing about mathematics for twenty years, she turned her attention to the needs of the poor and aged, with whom she died at the age of 81 in 1799.

Contributions:

Agnesi's greatest contribution to mathematics was her exceptionally clear and well-written calculus text, *Instituzioni Analitiche*, (*Foundations of Analysis*). This two-volume book systematically presented algebra, analytic geometry, calculus, and differential equations in a way that young readers could understand.

Anecdotes:

A Child Prodigy

At five years of age, Maria Agnesi amazed her family by becoming fluent in French. At nine, she demonstrated a remarkable grasp of Latin, Hebrew, and Greek. By the time she was 11, she was fluent in seven languages. She wrote a highly respected argument, in Latin, about the need for higher education for women. This essay was published when she was nine years old.

Friday Night Live

Agnesi's father, a mathematics professor, was eager to display his daughter's unusual abilities. When Maria was about 15, her father began to invite his intellectual friends and acquaintances to the Agnesi home for Friday night "academic evenings." Maria would prepare a discourse on some abstract philosophical or mathematical topic, and the men would engage in discussion with her and each other. Her younger sister, Teresa, an accomplished musician, provided intermission entertainment on the harpsichord.

Stories of these meetings spread. Soon they were attended by some of the most brilliant men throughout Europe. Many of them delighted in quizzing Maria in their own languages and hearing her respond in their languages without hesitation.

Maria, however, was shy; she found these evenings distasteful. Finally, when she was 21, she persuaded her father to excuse her.

Sleep Solves the Problem

Maria Agnesi often worked late into the night on mathematical problems. Sometimes she crawled into bed exhausted, frustrated by her inability to find the right approach to the problem. In the morning, she frequently found a complete and accurate solution on her desk—in her own handwriting.

This mystery was finally explained by her sisters, who saw her rise in her sleep, light the lamp, go to the desk and work. In the morning, Maria had no memory of these episodes, and usually was surprised by the methods she had used to find the solutions.

Her family was proud to tell the story of their "Somnambulist Sister."

A Convent Calling and Compromise

When she was about 20, Maria Agnesi asked her father's permission to join a convent. She felt tremendous compassion for the elderly poor in her community and wanted to help them.

Professor Agnesi loved his daughter, but he would not give in to this request. To console her, however, he promised to grant her three wishes. Her father was wealthy, and Maria might have asked for expensive gifts. Instead, she asked 1) to be allowed to dress simply and modestly, as a nun might, 2) to be allowed to go to church whenever she wished, and 3) to be excused from attending balls, the theater, and other social occasions.

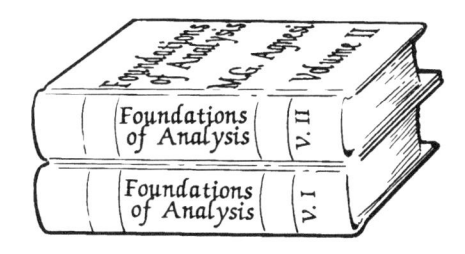

Teaching Leads to a Text

When Maria was about 14, her mother died, and Maria assumed many of the household responsibilities. Later, she was given the task of tutoring her younger brothers in mathematics. She was frustrated by the lack of appropriate books for them. The available texts were too complicated or too confusing.

This frustration prompted Agnesi to begin work on a text in mathematics that would help young readers discover good problem-solving approaches. She wanted to show how all of mathematics fits together. After almost ten years of work, her book was ready for printing. It was published in two volumes, totaling 1070 pages.

The response to Agnesi's text was phenomenal. Scholars from around the world praised its clarity and comprehensive scope. The book explained algebra, analytic geometry, calculus, and differential equations. The French Academy said, "There is no other book, in any language, that would enable a reader to penetrate as deeply, or as rapidly, into the fundamental concepts of analysis."

Where's the Witch?

For 50 years, Agnesi's book was considered the best mathematics textbook. She had written it in Italian, but it was soon translated into many other languages. John Colson, professor at Cambridge, learned Italian just so he could translate Agnesi's book for British youth.

One of the most fascinating and most original concepts in Agnesi's book is her study of a famous curve, called a "versiera" in Italian. This word was derived from the Latin word meaning "to turn," but "versiera" was also an abbreviation for the expression that means "wife of the devil" or "female goblin."

When Colson translated the book, he mistakenly called the curve the "witch" curve, and the name stuck. Because of this translation error, one of the kindest women in the history of mathematics is often referred to as "The 'Witch' of Agnesi."

Praised by the Pope

Agnesi's book won her many honors and gifts. It had been dedicated to Empress Maria Theresa. In appreciation, the Empress sent Agnesi a beautiful diamond ring and a small crystal box embedded with diamonds and other precious stones.

The greatest and most prized honor for Agnesi, however, was the recognition she received from Pope Benedict XIV. The pope himself was interested in mathematics, and corresponded with Agnesi through letters. He sent her a diamond studded wreath and a gold medal proclaiming her an "honorary lecturer" at the University of Bologna.

Dedicated to Service

Agnesi might have gone on in mathematics and taught in the university, but she chose instead to dedicate her life to helping the poor and ill. At first she volunteered her time to visit and to distribute medicine and food. Later, she gave her own room as a shelter for the homeless.

When a home for the needy was opened in Milan, Agnesi became one of the directors. She moved to the institution herself so she could be closer to her work. She sold the jewels and gold given her by the Empress and the Pope, and donated the funds to help the elderly. She gladly gave the rest of her life to console and comfort the sick and dying.

A Lasting Monument

When Agnesi died in 1799, she was 81 years old. At her request, she was buried in an unmarked grave with 15 other elderly women. No monument marks the spot.

On the 100th anniversary of her death, however, the city of Milan paid tribute to Agnesi by renaming several streets in her honor. A school bears her name and Agnesi scholarships are given to deserving girls.

Agnesi was a remarkable woman who showed that one can make important contributions to the world in more than one way. She influenced the development of mathematics by helping many students understand and enjoy their studies, and she also made the world a kinder place for others.

THE WITCH OF AGNESI

A curve studied by Maria Agnesi is commonly called "The Witch of Agnesi." This unusual name resulted from an incorrect translation from Italian to English. The curve has intrigued mathematicians since Agnesi because of its mathematical properties and its applications in physics.

A special case of "The Witch of Agnesi" curve is given by the equation

$$Y = \frac{64}{x^2 + 16}$$

Find some points described by this equation by completing the table. Then plot these points on the graph to determine the shape of this curve.

Use a calculator and round Y values to the nearest tenth.

X	Y
-8	
-7	
-6	
-5	
-4	
-3	
-2	
-1	
0	
1	
2	
3	
4	
5	
6	
7	
8	

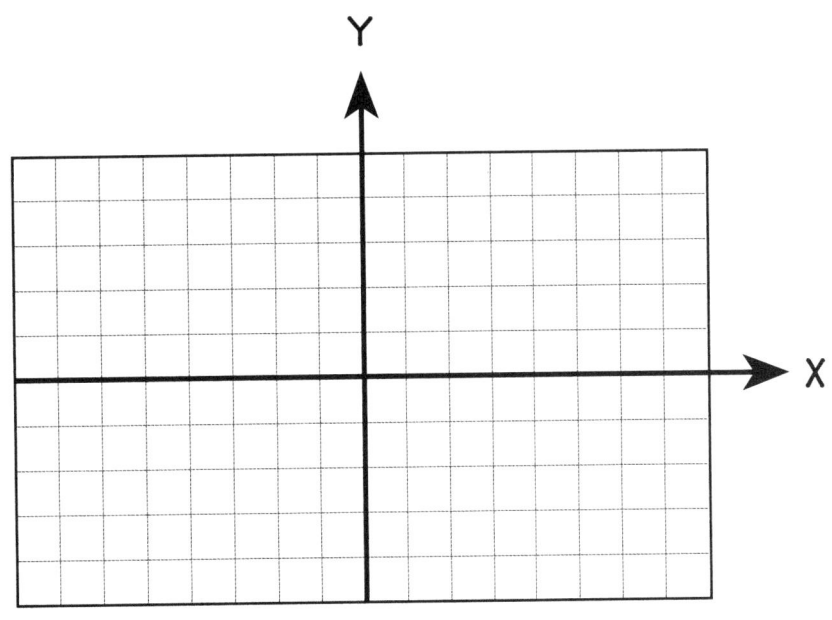

Questions:
1) What is the value of Y when X = 50?

2) Do you think the curve will ever cross the X-axis? Why or why not?

HISTORICAL CONNECTIONS VOL. III

EXPLORING ISOPERIMETRIC FIGURES

Maria Agnesi (1718-1799) taught her younger brothers geometry and wrote a textbook to help all young people understand it better. Here is a problem that intrigued Agnesi and many others.

The figures below are isoperimetric—that is, each one has the same perimeter. For this activity, the perimeter of each figure is 72 feet.

The areas of these figures, however, are all different!

Before doing any calculating, guess which figure has the largest area. Now compute the area of each figure. Record the areas in a list, ordering them from largest to smallest. Was your guess correct?

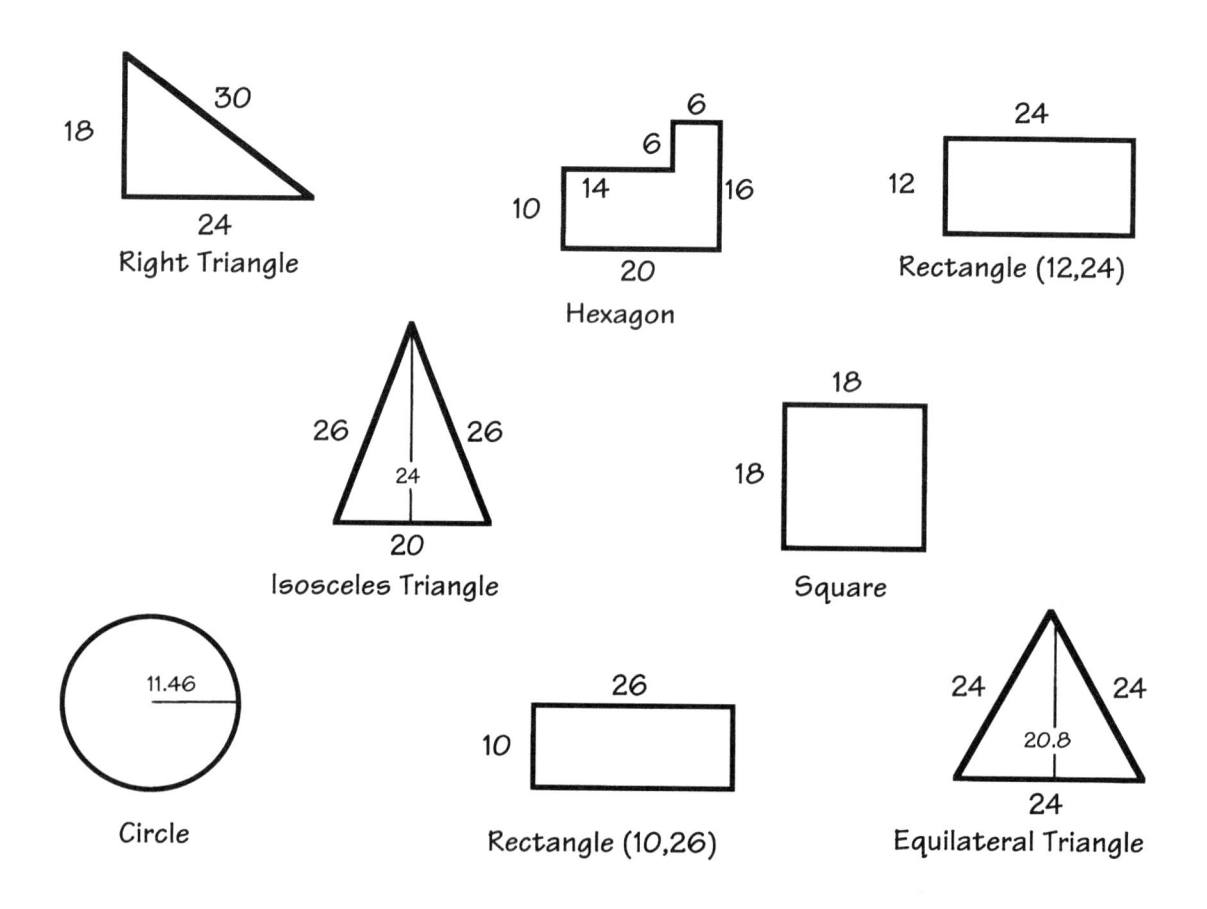

Right Triangle — 18, 30, 24

Hexagon — 6, 6, 14, 10, 16, 20

Rectangle (12,24) — 24, 12

Isosceles Triangle — 26, 26, 24, 20

Square — 18, 18

Circle — 11.46

Rectangle (10,26) — 26, 10

Equilateral Triangle — 24, 24, 24, 20.8

HISTORICAL CONNECTIONS VOL. III   © 2010 AIMS Education Foundation

X's, Y's, and Zzzzzzz's
A Skit to Read

Mr. Agnesi: You have certainly made me very proud, Maria.

Maria: Thank you, Father. I am fortunate to have a father who enjoys learning and thinking as much as I do.

Mr. Agnesi: You are so good at discussing philosphy and mathematics. I can't believe that **my** daughter is impressing the smartest men in the world!

Teresa: And Maria can communicate with the scholars in almost any language. Weren't you speaking seven languages fluently by the time you were 11 years old, Maria?

Mr. Agnesi: Yes, your sister Maria has proven that women can be very intelligent.

Maria: I believe, Father, that women need more opportunities to study and learn. If they had the chance, there are many other women who would enjoy learning as much as I do. Perhaps there are some women who could attend our Friday academic meetings.

Mr. Agnesi: Nonsense, my dear.

Narrator 1: Mr. Agnesi wouldn't think of allowing anything to distract attention from his daughter, Maria. He knew that her great intellectual ability would soon be the talk of Europe!

Narrator 2: But Maria was actually very shy. She didn't always enjoy the academic conversations. She loved to learn and study, but there were other things that she thought were also very important One night, after a Friday night meeting, Maria hoped her sister was still awake.

Maria: Teresa? Are you asleep?

Teresa: Almost.... What do you need?

Maria: I want to ask you a question. Do you think Father will always make me discuss ideas in front of important men? I'm getting so tired of it.

Teresa: You should be happy that he's so proud of you, Maria.

Maria: Too proud, I think. Doesn't he care about what I want to do? There's so much about me that he doesn't understand.

Teresa: If you feel strongly about this, you should tell him. Father is a reasonable man. It sounds like you will be unhappy if you don't at least try.

Maria: You're right, as usual. I will talk to him tomorrow.

Teresa: Good, only I'm not so sure you should tell him about your dreams of working with the poor. He may be reasonable, but he is also proud and stubborn.

Maria: I know I must be patient. Speaking of patience, this mathematics problem is wearing me out. I've been working on it for days!

Teresa: (with panic in her voice) You're not going to work on it now, are you? Maria?

Narrator 1: But Teresa was too late. Maria was already hunched over her desk, working furiously on the problem. Her pen scratched on the paper as she mumbled to herself.

Maria: How can this not work? I've done everything correctly.... Maybe if I reverse the process...

Teresa: Maria, please come to bed. It's so late! You'll be able to think more clearly in the morning.

Narrator 2: Maria sighed. She hated going to sleep with an unfinished problem on her desk, but she had no choice. She was stumped. Frustrated, Maria blew out the lamp and crawled into bed.

Narrator 1: The next morning, Maria heard Teresa getting clothes out of her closet. She stretched and then groaned as she remembered the unfinished problem waiting on her desk.

Teresa: Good morning, Maria. And congratulations!

Maria: Congratulations for what?

Teresa: For solving the problem! I'm sorry it took half the night for you to do it, but at least you found the solution.

Maria: What are you talking about?

Narrator 2: Maria jumped out of bed and stared in disbelief at the paper on her desk. The solution to the problem was circled at the bottom of the page!

Maria: Did you do this, Teresa? Is this your idea of a joke?

Teresa: Me? Maria, you know I could never do a problem like that!

Narrator 1: Maria studied the solution again. It **was** her handwriting, but how could it be? She had gone to bed at the same time as Teresa.

Maria: Teresa, when I went to bed the problem was unsolved. I slept all night! How could it be solved now?

Teresa: Don't you remember, Maria? You went to bed for a few hours, but then you got up. You lit the lamp, sat in your chair, and went to work on the problem. After awhile, you blew out the lamp and crawled back into bed. I hope you're not too tired today, Maria!

Narrator 2: But Maria didn't hear her sister. She was deep in thought, trying to remember the night, but she couldn't. How she could have solved such a difficult problem in her sleep, she wondered.

Maria: Can this solution possibly be right? I may have been sleepwalking, but surely I can't do mathematics in my sleep!

Narrator 1: Maria did the computations and checked her work from the night before. There were so many numbers that it took her awhile to figure it out, but finally she set her pen down. She turned to her sister, who had been waiting patiently.

Maria: Teresa! It's correct!

Maria's Puzzle

ACROSS
2 The mistaken name of the curve Agnesi studied.
5 Another name for older people.
6 Agnesi's book explained this subject.
9 A translation made this a "witch."
11 Agnesi's sister.
13 Day of the week Agnesi met with scholars.
14 What Agnesi wanted to be.
15 Church leader who liked mathematics and encouraged Agnesi.
16 Agnesi dedicated her life to help these people.
19 Agnesi believed women should be _____ .
20 Condition in which Agnesi sometimes solved problems.
21 The empress sent Agnesi one to wear.
23 Occupation of Agnesi's father.

DOWN
1 A place for homeless people.
3 The country where Agnesi was born.
4 The Pope gave Agnesi a gold_____.
7 Kind of box the empress gave Agnesi.
8 Number of languages Agnesi spoke.
9 Place where nuns live.
10 Agnesi wrote this to help her brothers.
12 Jewels sent to Agnesi from the empress.
14 Age of Agnesi when her first article was published.
17 Opposite of poor.
18 Agnesi's book was dedicated to her.
22 Agnesi received a jeweled_____.

Lagrange
1736 - 1813

JOSEPH L. LAGRANGE
MAKING MEASUREMENT METRIC

Biographical Facts:

Joseph Louis Lagrange was a French mathematician born in Turin, Italy, on January 25, 1736. He was the youngest of 11 children, and the only one to survive past early childhood. Although Lagrange became an excellent teacher, he remained modest and shy. He dedicated most of his time to teaching in Turin, Berlin, and Paris. Lagrange died in 1813 at the age of 77.

Contributions:

Lagrange's two greatest contributions to mathematics are generally considered to be his work in the calculus of variations and the development of the metric system. He was also interested in number theory and astronomy. Although he wrote on many subjects, his most significant publication was *Analytical Mechanics*.

Quotations by Lagrange:

"I do not know."

"I have always observed that the pretensions of all people are in exact inverse ratio to their merits."

"A mathematician has not fully understood his own work until he can effectively explain it to the first man he meets in the street."

Anecdotes:
Mixed-Up Measurement

In the late 18th century, merchants, surveyors, government officials, and common citizens throughout Europe became frustrated by the lack of uniform standards of weights and measures. In France, practically every district had its own system, making it difficult to do business. There were over 300 ways of measuring area alone.

Finally, the French government decided to do something about it. Joseph Lagrange was appointed head of the Committee on Weights and Measures. He persuaded his fellows to adopt a plan using a decimal system.

The committee agreed that a meter should equal one ten-millionth of the distance from the North Pole to the Equator. The standard mass of a gram would be determined by the mass of one cubic centimeter of distilled water at 4° Celsius.

Developing the metric system was a difficult, complex task, but it dramatically simplified scientific computation and improved communication throughout the world. What began in France was soon adopted throughout Europe as the most efficient and convenient way to measure length, mass, and volume.

Professor par Excellence

When the prestigious École Polytechnique opened in Paris in 1794, Joseph Lagrange was appointed the first professor of mathematics. The school quickly gained a reputation as the best place to study mathematics and science.

Lagrange was an excellent teacher. At first, the students were surprised by his appearance. He was just average in height, with small, pale blue eyes, and he seemed nervous and timid. But when he began to teach, they saw him differently. Lagrange was unusually humble. He often said "I do not know" when faced with a perplexing question. He was especially gifted at understanding the confusion that students felt, and he was always patient and clear in his explanations.

Surprised by Sophie

When École Polytechnique opened, women were not allowed to attend. But Sophie Germain, a brilliant young woman living in Paris, got her friends to share their notes from Lagrange's class. When Lagrange asked his students to hand in an original project, Sophie submitted one too. She signed it with a fictitious man's name, "Monsieur LeBlanc."

Of all the projects he collected, Lagrange was most impressed with the one by Monsieur LeBlanc. But the young "gentleman" never appeared in class. Finally, Lagrange discovered the secret about Sophie. Instead of being angry, he went personally to her home and encouraged Sophie to continue her mathematical study.

The Four Square Theorem

Lagrange had a special talent for number theory. He utilized his interests to solve a problem that had perplexed mathematicians for over 1500 years.

The question was this: Can every positive integer be expressed as the sum of four or fewer squares?

$$NUM = \Box + \Box + \Box + \Box$$

Diophantus (c. 250) assumed that every positive integer could be expressed this way, but he never explicitly stated the theorem.

Bachet (1581) verified that it was true for positive integers up to 325, but he was unable to prove it.

Descartes (1596) said that it was probably true but the proof might be "so difficult that I dared not undertake to find it."

Euler (1707) made progress but he was unable to complete the proof.

Finally, in 1770, Lagrange succeeded in constructing the first proof. Today, this is known as Lagrange's Four Square Theorem.

LAGRANGE'S FOUR SQUARE THEOREM

Joseph Lagrange, an 18th century French mathematician, was the first person to prove that every positive integer is expressible as a sum of four or fewer square numbers. This is known as Lagrange's Four Square Theorem.

Here are some examples. Note that 37 has more than one representation.

$$7 = 4 + 1 + 1 + 1$$
$$11 = 9 + 1 + 1$$
$$37 = 36 + 1 \text{ or } 16 + 16 + 4 + 1$$

Express the following positive integers as the sum of four or fewer squares to illustrate Lagrange's Four Square Theorem. Some numbers have more than one representation. Watch for emerging patterns.

1 =	13 =	25 =
2 =	14 =	26 =
3 =	15 =	27 =
4 =	16 =	28 =
5 =	17 =	29 =
6 =	18 =	30 =
7 =	19 =	48 =
8 =	20 =	56 =
9 =	21 =	77 =
10 =	22 =	87 =
11 =	23 =	92 =
12 =	24 =	114 =

1. Which of the integers from 10 to 20 have more than one representation when expressed as the sum of four or fewer squares? (Differing order does not count as a new representation.)

2. Attempt to write each of the integers from 1 to 20 as a sum of <u>three</u> or fewer squares. For which of these numbers can this not be done?

3. Express the year you were born as a sum of four or fewer squares.

SQUARE NUMBERS

1   4   9   16   25   36   49   64   81   100 …

HISTORICAL CONNECTIONS VOL. III © 2010 AIMS Education Foundation

PREDICTABLE PRODUCTS

The French mathematician Lagrange (1736-1813) worked in the area of mathematics called number theory. Square numbers intrigued him; perhaps he would have enjoyed this activity.

Multiply 4 Consecutive Numbers	Product	Product Plus 1	Written as a Square
1 x 2 x 3 x 4	24	25	5^2
2 x 3 x 4 x 5			
3 x 4 x 5 x 6			
4 x 5 x 6 x 7			
5 x 6 x 7 x 8			
6 x 7 x 8 x 9			
7 x 8 x 9 x 10			

Examine your completed table and make some generalizations. What pattern might be observed in the right column?
Use what you have discovered to predict the numbers in the right column below.

30 x 31 x 32 x 33			
50 x 51 x 52 x 53			
n(n + 1) (n + 2) (n + 3)			

Do you think the product plus 1 will always be a square number? Why?

The Metric Highway

Lagrange, a 17th century French mathematician, played a major role in promoting the use of the metric system. In this activity you will discover an interesting relationship between the kilometer and the mile.

Discover the pattern and complete the table.

Miles	Kilometers
10	10 + 5 + 1 = 16
20	20 + 10 + 2 = 32
30	30 + 15 + 3 = 48
40	40 + 20 + 4 = 64
50	
60	
70	
80	
90	
100	
200	
n	

Lagrange City
40 mi
64 km

HISTORICAL CONNECTIONS VOL. III © 2010 AIMS Education Foundation

Metric Crossword

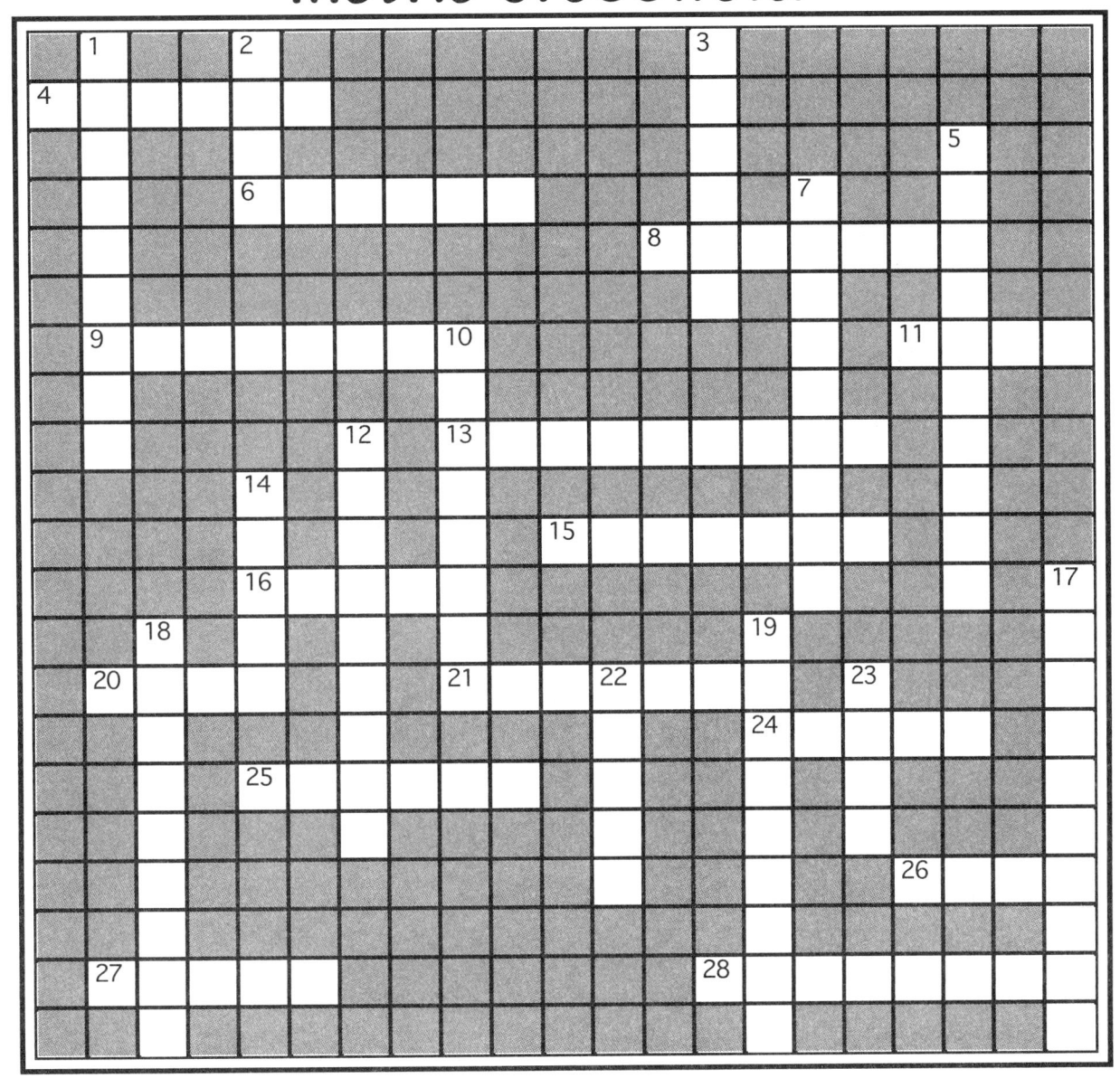

ACROSS
- 4 Twenty decimeters equal two_____.
- 6 Many countries use this system of measurement.
- 8 Metric measurements are converted by moving the_____.
- 9 One gram equals one _____ milligrams.
- 11 Prefix meaning one thousand.
- 13 One thousand liters equal one _____.
- 15 One hectoliter equals one _____ liters.
- 16 Standard unit used to measure capacity.
- 20 Prefix meaning one-tenth.
- 21 The word "meter" means _____.
- 24 Prefix meaning one-hundredth.
- 25 Country where the metric system was first developed.
- 26 One meter equals one ten-millionth of the distance from the north ___ to the equator.
- 27 Standard unit used to measure distance.
- 28 He helped develop the metric system.

DOWN
- 1 One-tenth of a meter equals one _____.
- 2 Standard unit used to measure weight.
- 3 Scientists developed the metric _____ of measurement in the 1700s.
- 5 One-thousandth of one liter equals one _____.
- 7 One thousand meters equal one_____.
- 10 Ten grams equal one _____.
- 12 One-hundredth of one gram equals one _____.
- 14 Prefix meaning one-thousandth.
- 17 One-hundredth of one meter equals one _____.
- 18 Ten liters equal one _____.
- 19 One hundred grams equal one _____.
- 22 Milligrams are used to measure objects that are very _____.
- 23 A liter is a ___ of measurement.

HISTORICAL CONNECTIONS VOL. III © 2010 AIMS Education Foundation

METRIC MANIA

Mathematician Joseph Lagrange worked with scientists in the 18th century to develop the metric system. Without actually measuring, use what you know of the metric system to guess the approximate measurements.

1. A newborn baby weighs about
   a. 3 kilograms
   b. 30 kilograms
   c. 300 kilograms

2. One penny weighs
   a. 3 grams
   b. 10 milligrams
   c. 13 kilograms

3. Some camera film is measured using
   a. meters
   b. millimeters
   c. kilometers

4. A regular size soft drink can holds
   a. 2 liters
   b. 1.5 liters
   c. 355 milliliters

5. A length of a pencil is about
   a. 15 meters
   b. 15 centimeters
   c. 15 millimeters

6. An eyedropper holds
   a. 200 milliliters
   b. 70 milliliters
   c. 6 milliliters

7. A soccer field should be measured using
   a. grams
   b. meters
   c. kiloliters

8. Two meters is about the height of
   a. a desk
   b. a ceiling
   c. a door

9. The length of a dollar bill is
   a. 16 millimeters
   b. 16 centimeters
   c. 1.6 meters

10. Once around a track is
    a. 4 meters
    b. 40 meters
    c. 400 meters

11. A CD weighs about
    a. 4 grams
    b. 14 grams
    c. 2 kilograms

12. Water in a small swimming pool should be measured using
    a. milliliters
    b. kiloliters
    c. liters

Somerville
1780 - 1872

MARY SOMERVILLE
THE QUEEN OF 19TH CENTURY SCIENCE

Biographical Facts:

Mary Fairfax Somerville was born December 26, 1780, in Burntisland, Scotland. Her father, a Scottish admiral, came from the same family line as George Washington. Except for one year of formal schooling, she was self-educated. After marrying William Somerville, she moved to London. There, and in her travels throughout Europe, she met other scientists and mathematicians. She spent her last 25 years in Italy, where she died in 1872 at the age of 92.

Contributions:

Mary Somerville made mathematics and science accessible to many people through her writing. Her first major project was a popularized version of *Celestial Mechanics* by Pierre Laplace. Very few people could understand the original. Somerville's book, called *Mechanisms of the Heavens*, made Laplace's ideas readable by a large audience. It became a popular text for courses in higher mathematics and astronomy.

Somerville wrote three additional books in various scientific fields. Each was well received and helped to shape the understanding of mathematics and science in the 19th century.

Quotation by Somerville:

"All of mathematics and science is interconnected."

Anecdotes:

A Wild Child

As a child, Mary Somerville loved her freedom. Girls in Scotland were not expected to go to school, so Mary spent her days caring for the family's poultry and exploring the tidepools on the seacoast near her home.

Once, when her father returned from a mission at sea, he decided Mary had grown too wild. She was enrolled at Miss Primrose's exclusive academy in Musselburgh.

Memorizing the Dictionary

Formal schooling did not agree with Mary Somerville. The girls were forced to wear restrictive braces to ensure proper posture. Teaching was unimaginative and creativity was not rewarded. Requiring each student to memorize a page of Johnson's dictionary was considered an effective educational practice. After one year, Mary's persistent tears persuaded her parents to let her return home.

Stargazing

Mary Somerville was a lonely child whose favorite companions were starfish, crabs, and birds. But she found solace sitting by the attic window, dreaming about the constellations. Later, when reading about navigation, she learned she would never fully understand the stars unless she studied mathematics. Gaining such knowledge became her compelling desire.

The Intriguing X and Y

In the early 1800s, ladies' fashion magazines occasionally interspersed puzzles and problems among their illustrations. One day when she and a friend were looking at such a magazine, Mary noticed a problem with X's and Y's in it. She wondered what they stood for, but all anyone could tell her was that it was called "algebra." Not until she overheard her younger brother being tutored in algebra did she learn what it was. Then, she begged the tutor to bring her books about algebra and geometry, which she quickly mastered.

A Life of Discipline

As Mary grew older, she established a daily pattern of discipline which she maintained throughout her life. She rose early each day to begin her chores and housework. She practiced piano four or five hours a day. She sewed all of her own clothes. She was an accomplished painter, and loved to dance. She taught herself Latin and, when books became available, she studied mathematics and physics.

Most of Mary's studying was done at night, when the house was quiet and her parents could not see her. Like most parents of the time, they believed that intense study was not healthy for young women. They tried confiscating her candles, but Mary simply memorized mathematical problems and solved them in her head in the dark.

Recognition at Last

Although Mary Somerville was not motivated by a desire for fame or fortune, her work was highly respected by other mathematicians and scientists. In 1835, she and Caroline Hershel were the first women elected to the Royal Astronomical Society. The King of England awarded her with an annual pension for her "eminence in science and literature." Sir Edward Parry, a leading astronomer in England, named an island in the Arctic after her. One of the first two women's colleges at Oxford was named Somerville College in her honor. When Mary Somerville died, *The London Post* called her "The Queen of Nineteenth-Century Science."

JUST PASSING THROUGH

A diagonal drawn in this 3 by 2 rectangle passes through four unit squares.

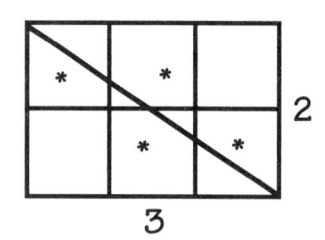

Use square grid paper to draw rectangles whose dimensions are listed in the table. Some are drawn for you. Count the number of unit squares a diagonal passes through. Enter your results in the table.

Discover the rule that gives the number of unit squares a diagonal passes through for an L by W rectangle. The greatest common divisor (GCD) of the length and width is used in this rule.

LENGTH L	WIDTH W	GCD OF L AND W	NO. OF UNIT SQUARES
3	2	1	4
3	1		
4	2		
5	3		
6	4		
6	3		
7	5		
Use your rule to answer the rest.			
100	75		
600	50		
300	200		

What rule did you discover?

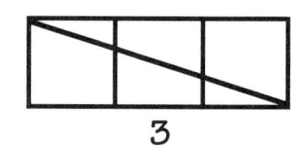

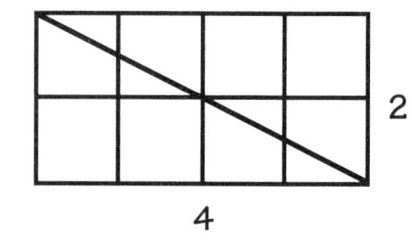

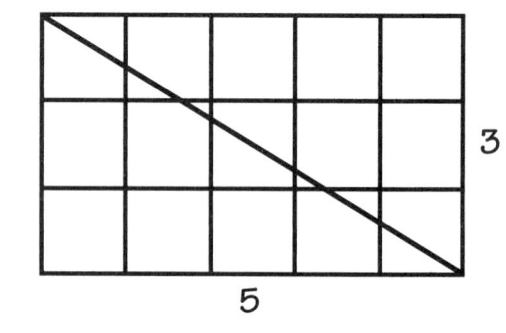

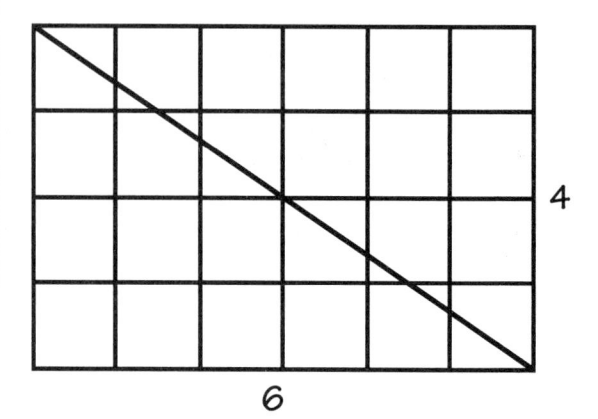

HISTORICAL CONNECTIONS VOL. III © 2010 AIMS Education Foundation

STAR SHAPES

Like many young people, Mary Somerville (a 19th century Scottish mathematician) preferred the outdoors. If she had to be inside, however, her favorite spot was an attic window seat where she could gaze at the stars to her heart's content. She said later that the constellations inspired her to study mathematics.

Suppose you plotted constellations on dot paper. A simple formula (known as Pick's Theorem) can help you determine the areas of these unusual figures. Let A equal the area of the figure, let B equal the number of dots on the boundary, and let I equal the number of dots in the interior of the figure.

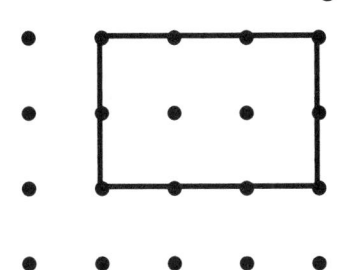

$$A = \frac{1}{2}B + I - 1$$

Consider the rectangle on the left. There are 10 dots on its boundary and two dots in its interior. Using Pick's Theorem, we see that A = 5 + 2 - 1 = 6.

With figures that look more like constellations, this method makes a difficult problem remarkably easy. Find the areas of these figures.

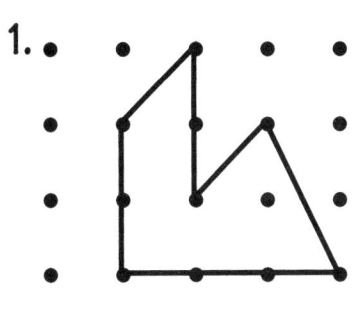

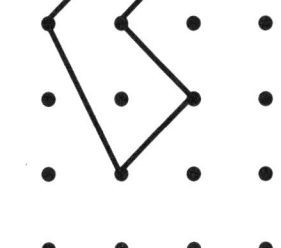

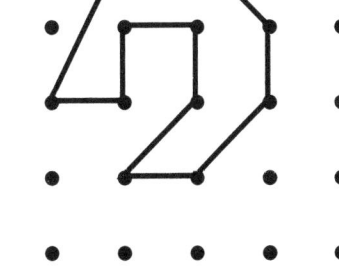

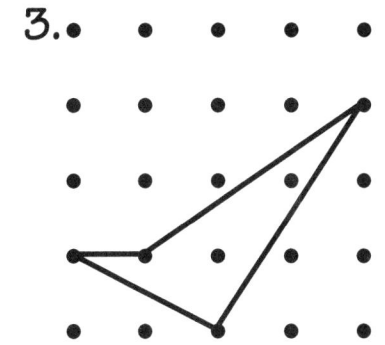

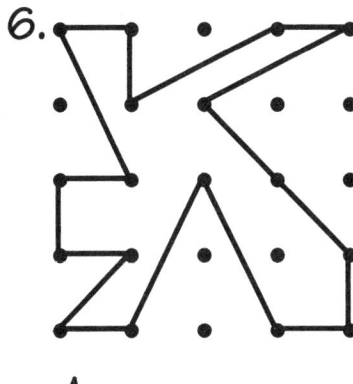

1. A =

2. A =

3. A =

4. A =

5. A =

6. A =

HISTORICAL CONNECTIONS VOL. III © 2010 AIMS Education Foundation

WHERE DOES THE OCEAN END?

Mary Somerville, a 19th century Scottish mathematician, grew up right next to the beach. She often played among the tide pools and searched the horizon for signs of her father's ships. As an adult, she studied navigation and marine biology as well as mathematics.

Have you ever stood on the beach and wondered how far you could see the ocean? Because the Earth is a sphere, the distance you can see the ocean is not very far.

Suppose a person 6 feet tall is standing on the beach. This drawing illustrates the person's line of sight.

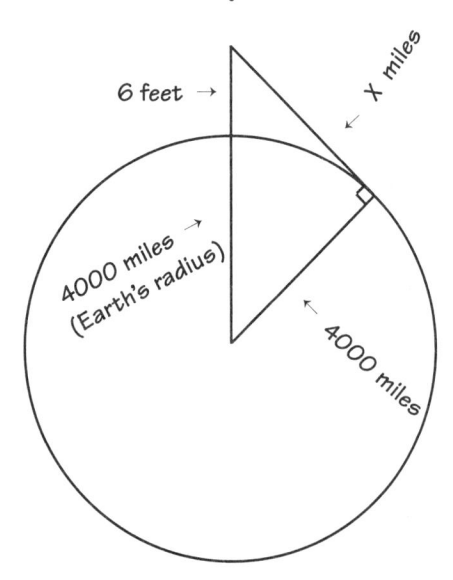

Using the Pythagorean theorem and your calculator, find how many miles of ocean can be seen by a person 6 feet tall.

Exercises:
1. Suppose Mary Somerville were standing on the beach as a child. When she was 4 feet tall, how far would she have been able to look across and see the ocean?

2. Suppose you were standing on a rock so that your eyes were 20 feet above sea level. How many miles of ocean surface would you be able to see?

3. Suppose you were on top of a lighthouse so that your eyes were 100 feet above sea level. How many miles of ocean surface would you be able to see?

AN ANT THERMOMETER

Mary Somerville, the Scottish mathematician, was also an avid student of nature. She loved observing the animals, birds, and insects near her coastal home.

Another scientist reported studies he had made of two species of ants called "line runners." They follow a fixed path along the ground, running as if they had no power to stop. The scientist found that within normal temperature ranges, the warmer it is, the faster these ants run. That is, there is a relationship between temperature and the speed of the ants.

By repeated experiments, the scientist accumulated data which is recorded on the right.

Discover the relationship between temperature and the speed of the ants by completing the table.

Temperature (Celsius)	Speed of Ants in Cm/Minute
13	8
14	16
15	24
16	32
17	
18	
19	
n	

HISTORICAL CONNECTIONS VOL. III © 2010 AIMS Education Foundation

Dodgson
1832 - 1898

CHARLES DODGSON
MATHEMATICIAN IN WONDERLAND

Biographical Facts:

Charles Lutwidge Dodgson, better known as Lewis Carroll, was born in Daresbury, in Cheshire, England, on January 27, 1832. The eldest of the local parish priest's eleven children, Dodgson was educated at home until the age of 12. He attended Christ Church College at Oxford, where he later taught mathematics. He became an expert amateur photographer. Dodgson never married, and died just before his 66th birthday, in 1898.

Contributions:

Charles Dodgson was a mathematician and logician. Although he taught for many years at Oxford, he is better known as a writer. He compiled texts for undergraduate students at Oxford, and wrote a considerable number of books on serious mathematical subjects, including historical mathematics.

Under the pen name of Lewis Carroll, he wrote the well-known *Alice's Adventures in Wonderland* and *Alice Through the Looking Glass*, as well as several collections of logic games and puzzles.

Anecdotes:

An Entertaining Child

Charles Dodgson was always shy, perhaps because of a very noticeable stammer in his speech. As a child, however, he entertained himself–and delighted his large family–with magic tricks, puppet shows, and humorous poems and stories.

The Original Alice

Dodgson enjoyed being with children. He loved talking with them and testing new puzzle ideas on them. One of his favorite children was Alice Liddell, daughter of the Dean of Christ Church College in Oxford, where Dodgson taught.

One day while Alice and her sister were boating with Dodgson, they begged him for a story. He began to tell an amazing story about "Alice," which the girls insisted he continue every time they were together. Several years later, he gave Alice Liddell a handwritten manuscript of the stories as a Christmas gift.

Dodgson's friends finally persuaded him to have Alice's stories published. They became *Alice's Adventures in Wonderland* and *Alice Through the Looking Glass*. The stories were immensely popular. Hidden within the stories are many mathematical concepts and ideas.

Taking a Pseudonym

Dodgson was not eager for publicity and fame. To ensure his privacy, he adopted a pseudonym: Lewis Carroll. He explained that this name came from his own first two names: Charles Lutwidge. First, he translated them into Latin, for "Carolus Lodovicus." Then he Anglicized the name to "Lewis Carroll."

An Embarrassing Entrance

Dodgson was a popular guest at children's parties. Once, when he was invited to a child's party in London, he decided to surprise the children at the party by crawling in on his hands and knees. Unfortunately, he accidentally crawled into the house next door, surprising a group of adults who were also having a party!

A Soft Spot for Animals

Charles Dodgson was a gentle, kind man. He did not like to see anyone suffer, including animals. When he learned of the cruel butchering processes used in England at that time, he campaigned for laws which would ensure animals a painless death.

One day when Dodgson was out walking, he found a little kitten with a fishhook caught in its mouth. He picked the furry kitten up, took it to a doctor, and held it while the hook was cut and removed. When the doctor learned that the kitten did not belong to Dodgson, he refused to charge for the treatment. Dodgson gently deposited the kitten back at the spot where he had found it, and continued his walk.

Fit for a Queen

Queen Victoria read Dodgson's two *Alice* books with delight. She summoned her courtier and placed an order. "Bring me all the books this man has written. I want to read every one!"

When the courtier returned several days later, the queen was surprised to see a tall stack of books. Unfortunately, she could not read or understand them, because most were on mathematical subjects!

This is Arithmetic?

One of Dodgson's great strengths as a writer was his wonderful way with words. Often, he used words to create a stinging wit. In one of his books, he describes the branches of arithmetic. Instead of addition, subtraction, multiplication, and division, Dodgson lists "Ambition, Distraction, Uglification, and Derision."

DODGSON'S DOUBLETS
A Problem-Solving Activity

Charles Dodgson, also known as Lewis Carroll, was a mathematician and storyteller. One day when several children complained that they were bored, he made up a new kind of puzzle called a "doublet." The youngsters liked the puzzles so much that Dodgson showed them to his adult friends, who also thought they were entertaining. Soon they were printed in magazines and books.

To solve a doublet puzzle you must change one word to another through a series of stages. Only one letter may be changed at a time and each change must result in a new word. For example, Dodgson may have challenged children to "put FOOT into SHOE," or "turn WET into DRY."

FOOT	WET
SOOT	BET
SHOT	BAT
SHOE	BAY
	DAY
	DRY

Have fun solving the following doublets. Try to create the new words with as few steps as possible. There is usually more than one way to reach the new word.

1. Raise SIX to TEN
2. Turn EAST into WEST
3. Sail BOAT into LAKE
4. Change MEAN to KIND
5. Make ADD into SUM
6. Shape SNOW into BALL
7. Change HATE into LOVE

It is fun to make up doublets. Create some for your friends to try.

DODGSON'S DISCOVERY

Toward the end of his life, Charles Dodgson (1832-1898) wrote in his diary that he had discovered a new fact about square numbers. Double the sum of two square numbers, he said, could always be expressed as the sum of two square numbers.

Remember, the square numbers are

1 4 9 16 25 36 49 64 81 100 121 144 . . .

Test Dodgson's discovery for yourself.

1. Choose any two square numbers.
2. Add these two numbers.
3. Double your result.
4. Now try to express your result as the sum of two squares.

First Square	Second Square	Sum of Squares Chosen	Double of Sum	Expressed as Sum of Two Squares
4	9	13	26	1 + 25
25	64	89	178	9 + 169
4	16			
9	25			
16	25			
36	49			
64	81			
4	36			
16	100			
64	121			

Choose other square numbers and continue to test them.

Do you think this will always work? Can you show that it will?

LIGHTHEARTED LOGIC

Charles Dodgson, who wrote *Alice in Wonderland* under the name of Lewis Carroll, was a great British mathematician. He often combined his interest in logic and his rich imagination to invent puzzles and games. Here is one of his famous logic puzzles.

You must accept each of the following statements as true. The object is to use all of the statements together to produce a single conclusion.

1. If an animal is in this house, then it is a cat.
2. If an animal loves to gaze at the moon, then it is suitable for a pet.
3. If I don't avoid an animal, then I don't detest them.
4. If an animal is carnivorous, then it prowls at night.
5. If an animal is a cat, then it kills mice.
6. If an animal takes to me, then it is in this house.
7. If an animal is suitable for a pet, then it is not a kangaroo.
8. If an animal kills mice, then it is carnivora.
9. If I don't detest them, then animals take to me.
10. If an animal prowls at night, then it loves to gaze at the moon.

What is the conclusion which must be reached if all ten of the statements are used?

MORE LOGIC PUZZLES

Charles Dodgson, the 19th century British mathematician, loved to think up logic puzzles to both challenge and entertain his students and friends. These two should challenge your logical thinking skills.

Assume each of the following statements is true. Use all of them to reach a *logical conclusion*.

1. If I get good grades, then I go to college.
2. If I get a good job, then I make a good salary.
3. If I stay home, then I study.
4. If I go to college, then I get a good job.
5. If it is raining, then I stay home.
6. If I study, then I get good grades.

What is a logical conclusion?

Here's another one:
1. If they wear old shoes, then the children wear holes in their socks.
2. If the sock business booms, then Joe can buy a new car.
3. If the pears are not growing, then the children are wearing old shoes.
4. If it freezes in September, then the pears do not grow.
5. If the children are wearing holes in their socks, then the sock business is booming.
6. If Joe has dates quite often, then all the young ladies are happy.
7. If Joe has a new car, then Joe has dates quite often.

What is a logical conclusion?

The Real Alice
A Skit to Read

Narrator 1: Once upon a time, in the town of Oxford, England, there lived a girl named Alice Liddell. Alice's father was the Dean of Christ Church College at Oxford. This meant that the whole family **lived** right on the campus.

Narrator 2: Alice found wonderful things to do during the days while her father worked. She and her sisters loved to play with dolls and toys in their playroom. Miss Prickett was their governess. She was nice but not much fun; she never liked to play games. Alice's favorite days were days when Mr. Charles Dodgson came to visit.

Mr. Dodgson: Good morning, Mrs. Liddell.

Mrs. Liddell: Good morning, Mr. Dodgson. How is the mathematics teacher today? Are your students doing well this term?

Mr. Dodgson: I'm fine, thank you, and they're doing well. I was wondering if I might take Alice and her sisters on a boat ride down the River Cherwell. It looks like it will be a lovely afternoon.

Mrs. Liddell: Oh, of course. I'm sure the girls would enjoy that very much. They always come back with the most wonderful stories of their adventures. And last time Alice brought a beautiful photograph you had taken of her. Thank you, Mr. Dodgson.

Narrator 3: Mr. Dodgson loved to take pictures. The camera had just been invented, so it was very special for Mr. Dodgson to own one. Although the Liddell children often squirmed and made the photographs blurry, they were much more fun to work with than adults. Alice, especially, was always a bundle of energy.

Mr. Dodgson: Be careful getting into the boat, girls. Watch your step! Edith, take your sister's hand and help her in.

Alice: I'm fine, Edith. There, see? I made it. And I would have been even faster if Mother hadn't made me wear this fancy dress.

Edith: Mr. Dodgson, Mother said you wanted to take pictures of us by the River Cherwell.

Mr. Dodgson: So that's why you're both so dressed up! Well, we can't let this pretty day and you pretty girls slip by without a photograph or two. After our boat ride, I'll get the camera.

Edith: We will try to sit very still for the camera, Mr. Dodgson.

Mr. Dodgson: Good. Last time you two were as wiggly as worms!

Narrator 1: The sisters giggled as Mr. Dodgson pretended he was a wiggly worm. They remembered the time he wanted to surprise some children at a party, so he had crawled like a bear through the front door.

Narrator 2: But poor Mr. Dodgson had gone to the wrong house and surprised a party of adults, not children! He was very embarrassed! The mistake was a funny

	story the Liddell children loved to tell. Alice always thought that Mr. Dodgson was the *best* storyteller.
Alice:	Pleeeease tell us another story, Mr. Dodgson. This time, make it even longer than yesterday's!
Mr. Dodgson:	Another story? Don't you girls ever get tired of stories?
Edith:	Not of your stories! Start the story now while we're in the boat and then when we get to our picnic spot you can continue.
Mr. Dodgson:	Oh, my. That would be a long story.
Alice:	Pleeeease, Mr. Dodgson! Please!
Mr. Dodgson:	Okay...all right. Let me think here...
Narrator 3:	Mr. Dodgson always made up the stories in his head. He never told anyone else's stories—his were all originals. Alice loved the stories, but she loved all his other games, too. Mr. Dodgson liked to play with puzzles and word games. When Mr. Dodgson was around, Alice's favorite words were "Let's pretend!" She knew that even though he was an adult, Mr. Dodgson would like that game, too.
Mr. Dodgson:	I've got it. Ready for the story, girls?
Alice:	Yes, we're very ready. Please begin!
Mr. Dodgson:	Once upon a time, there was a girl named Alice...
Alice:	Me? Is this story about me?
Mr. Dodgson:	You'll have to listen to the rest of the story to find out.
Edith:	Keep going, Mr. Dodgson. If it is about Alice, it promises to be an adventure!
Alice:	You must promise to write down this story, Mr. Dodgson. It must be about me!
Narrator 1:	Mr. Dodgson did as Alice begged and wrote the story. Mr. Dodgson gave Alice a handwritten copy of *Alice's Adventures in Wonderland*. Although he used the pretend name Lewis Carroll when the story was published, it was really Mr. Charles Dodgson, the mathematics teacher, who wrote the story. And Alice Liddell, we all know, was the **real** Alice.

Venn
1834 - 1923

JOHN VENN
DIAGRAM DESIGNER

Biographical Facts:

John Venn was a British mathematician, philosopher, and clergyman who lived from 1834 to 1923. He was a Fellow of Gonville and Caius College, Cambridge, from 1857 until his death. During his last 20 years, he was president of the college.

Venn married Susanna Carnegie in 1867. They had one son, John Archibald, who became president of Queen's College, Cambridge, in 1932.

Contributions:

Venn's most important work was in logic and probability. His books, *Logic of Chance, Empirical Logic,* and *Symbolic Logic,* were highly esteemed texts in the late 19th and early 20th centuries. In *Symbolic Logic*, he introduced the diagrams that bear his name. Venn diagrams have dramatically clarified and simplified many important ideas in mathematics and logic.

Anecdotes:

Heritage Reigns

The Venn family shared a deep respect for both education and religion. Young John was brought up rather rigidly in the family tradition. There was no question about where he would attend college. He proudly represented the eighth generation to attend Cambridge.

Just for Fun

As a boy, Venn was interested in botany and mechanics. These remained hobbies throughout his life. He was an avid walker and mountain climber who treasured his opportunities to observe and learn about nature. In 1909, he proudly showed friends a mechanical bowling machine he had designed and built.

Following Tradition

After attending two London schools, Venn entered Gonville and Caius College, Cambridge, in 1853. He received his degree in mathematics in 1857 and was elected a fellow of his college, a position he held until his death.

In 1859, Venn followed family tradition by taking holy orders. He served as priest in several communities, but was frequently torn by his interest in philosophy. He felt that some of his questioning and study might test the Anglican dogma he was supposed to represent. Finally, in 1883, he resigned from his church roles and went back to Cambridge to teach at Gonville and Caius. Throughout his life, however, Venn remained a devout believer and active church member.

Professional Interests

At Gonville and Caius, Venn lectured, researched, and wrote on a wide range of topics. Fascinated by historical records, Venn wrote a comprehensive history of Gonville and Caius College. He painstakingly compiled and methodically recorded alumni records. He also wrote several journals of his family's history.

Venn devoted 30 years to the study and teaching of logic, at first paying special attention to probability. His work in these areas made a dramatic impact.

Venn Designs Diagrams

In his book, *Symbolic Logic,* Venn showed how a number of closed curves, such as circles, could be used to represent sets with something in common. These diagrams—now called Venn diagrams—graphically illustrate the relationships between these sets and the subsets that arise from them.

Who would have ever thought that the drawing of several overlapping circles could so dramatically and powerfully simplify so many important ideas in mathematics and logic?

At their simplest levels, Venn diagrams are useful for showing children how to count. They may also be used by computer programmers to design logic circuits. Perhaps the most important role of Venn diagrams is to reduce the confusion resulting from language. Many problems which sound complex become simple through the use of the diagrams. Venn diagrams help to organize information so that it can be visualized and understood.

Venn diagrams may be drawn in many different configurations. Usually, the universal set is represented by a rectangle. Other sets of interest within the universal set are represented by circular or oval regions that may or may not intersect.

Letting in the Light

As a memorial to Venn, a stained glass window representing Venn diagrams has been mounted in the Hall of Gonville and Caius College.

PROBLEM SOLVING USING VENN DIAGRAMS

Venn diagrams, developed by Englishman John Venn (1834-1923), are a powerful problem-solving tool. Use the Venn diagrams provided to solve the following problems. Write the appropriate numbers in each region.

Problem 1

Student athletes were surveyed to see whether they played basketball, soccer, or both. Of 100 students surveyed,

56 played basketball
24 played both basketball and soccer
68 played soccer

How many played basketball only?

How many played soccer only?

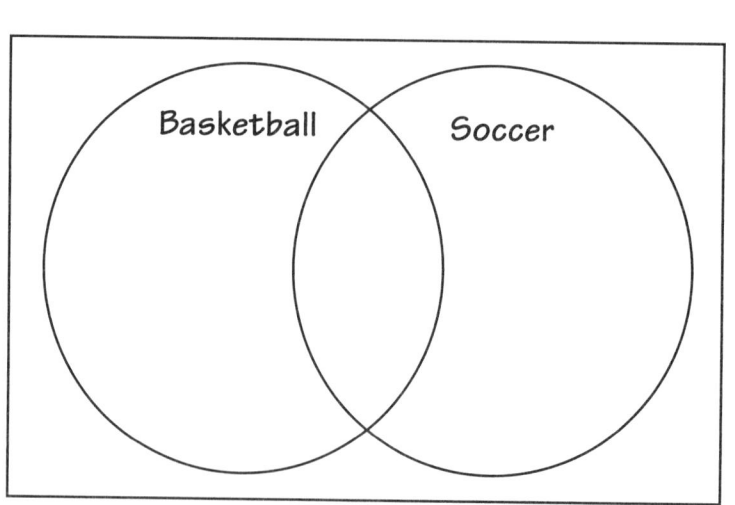

Problem 2

A school is taking three music organizations to a festival.

30 students sing in the choir
40 students play in the orchestra
50 students march in the band
15 students belong to the choir and the orchestra
10 students belong to the orchestra and the band
14 students belong to the choir and the band
5 students belong to all three groups

How many students will need seats on the bus?

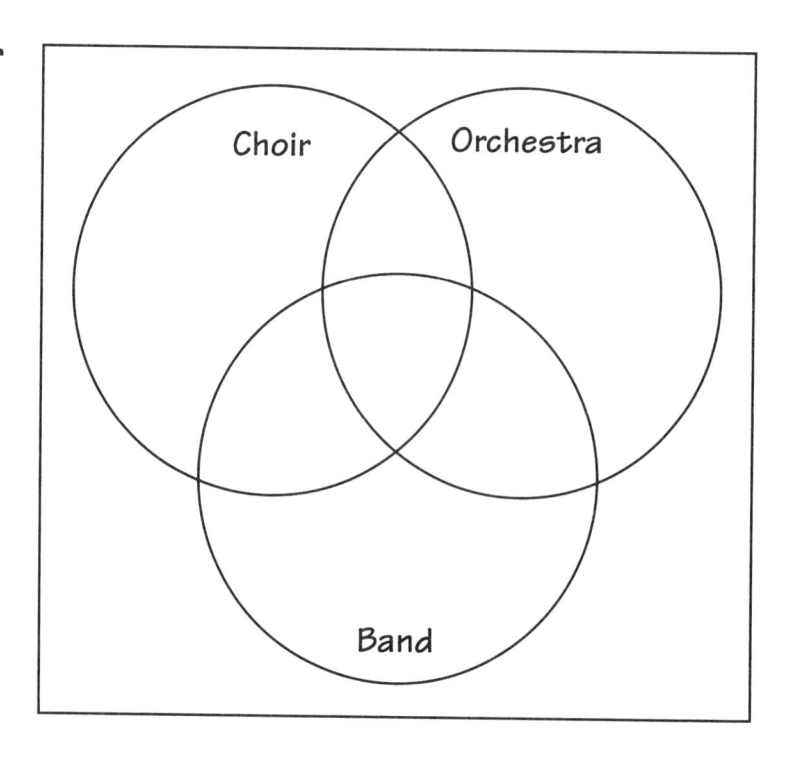

VENN DIAGRAMS SOLVE THE PROBLEM

Write the appropriate numbers in each region of the Venn diagrams provided to solve the problems.

Problem 1
Three popular courses at MacArthur Junior High are geography, art, and science. A review of the schedules of 200 students showed that
- 70 have geography
- 80 have science
- 60 have art
- 35 have geography and science
- 33 have geography and art
- 31 have science and art
- 15 have geography, science, and art

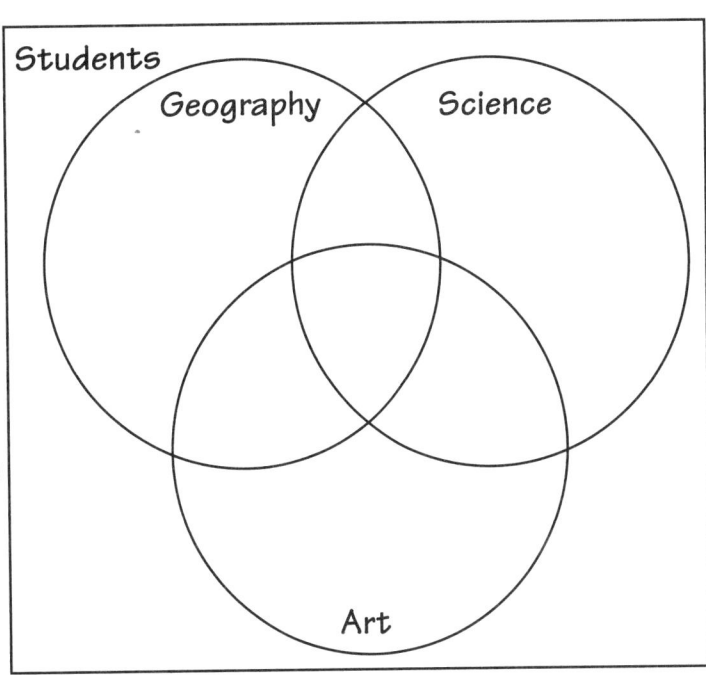

How many of the 200 students have none of these courses?

Problem 2
Ms. Wilson gave her algebra students three optional problems (A, B, and C) for extra credit. She calculated that
- 54% of the students did problem A
- 45% did B
- 36% did C
- 12% did A and B
- 17% did B and C
- 20% did A and C
- 5% did all three (A, B, and C)

What percent of the students did not turn in any of the problems?

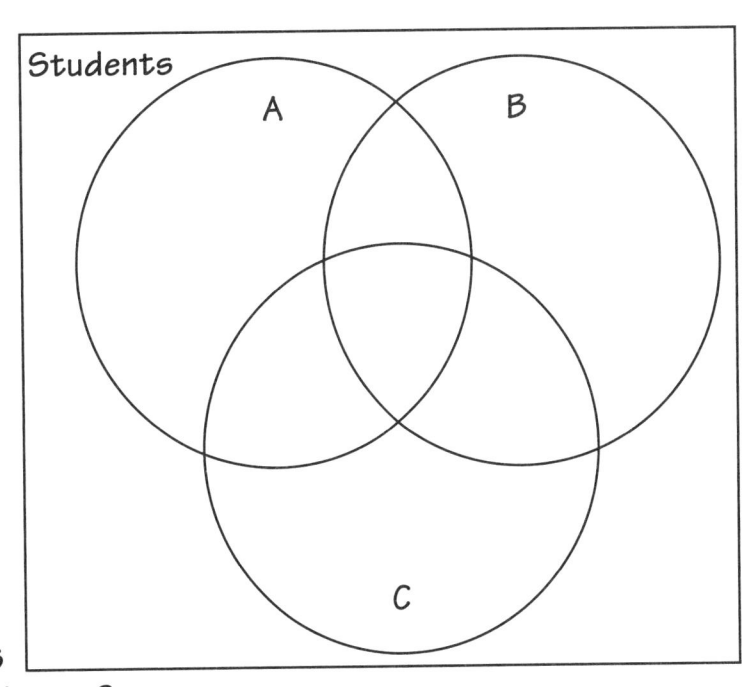

HISTORICAL CONNECTIONS VOL. III

WHO'S IN CHARGE?

Use these clues to identify the position of each member in an office complex. Check off positions people cannot hold in the grid below.

1. Fred and the assistant manager enjoy fishing together.
2. Adam, Susan, the manager, and the computer programmer all graduated from the same college.
3. John and the secretary are the same age.
4. Sam and the clerk are neighbors of the manager.
5. Adam and Sam surprised the assistant manager on his birthday.
6. John, Fred, and the manager enjoy bowling.
7. The computer programmer is related to Fred.
8. Susan and the clerk are neighbors.
9. John and the computer programmer graduated from the same high school.
10. John, Adam, and the cashier enjoy watching baseball.
11. Susan and the assistant manager enjoy reading during their leisure time.
12. Adam, Susan, and the secretary attend the same church.

	John	Susan	Fred	Adam	Mary	Sam
Manager						
Assistant Manager						
Cashier						
Secretary						
Clerk						
Computer Programmer						

CROSSING THE RIVER

British mathematician John Venn wrote about the power of logical thinking. Use logic to solve this famous old puzzle.

Once there was a showman traveling on foot with a wolf, a goat, and a cabbage. When they came to a wide river, the showman paused to think. A small boat was available for his use, but it would hold only himself and one of the others. He could take the wolf, the goat, or the cabbage, but not more than one at a time.

The showman's problem was complicated by the nature of his companions. He dare not leave the wolf alone with the goat or the goat alone with the cabbage. Given a chance, the wolf would eat the goat! If the showman turned his back, the goat would eat the cabbage!

After thinking for awhile, the showman realized that it was possible to use the boat to transport himself and all of his belongings safely across the river.

How did he do it?

ROWING RELAY

John Venn, the British mathematician, enjoyed developing problems to exercise logical thinking skills.

Suppose a team competition takes place at the local lake. The goal is to get a team of four persons across the lake in as little time as possible.

The teams must obey several rules. They must never have more than two persons in the boat, and the *slower* person in the boat must always do the rowing.

In timed trials, the Yellow team has determined the rowing times for their members:

Member A: 20 minutes
Member B: 15 minutes
Member C: 10 minutes
Member D: 5 minutes

What is the minimum time in which the Yellow team could get its entire team to the other side of the lake?

How should they organize themselves to achieve this minimum?

The Red team members can row in these times:

Member A: 25 minutes
Member B: 20 minutes
Member C: 10 minutes
Member D: 5 minutes

What is the minimum time in which the Red team could get to the other side of the lake?

How should they do it?

Noether
1882 - 1935

EMMY NOETHER
CHANGING THE FACE OF ALGEBRA

Biographical Facts:

Amalie "Emmy" Noether (NUR-ter) was born in Erlangen, Germany, on March 23, 1882. Her father, Max, was a mathematics professor at the local university. She caught his love of mathematics and went on to earn a Ph.D. in spite of limited opportunities for women in the field. In 1933, after being forced to leave Germany, she taught at Bryn Mawr College, near Philadelphia. She died in 1935 from complications following routine surgery.

Contributions:

Emmy Noether is one of the leading figures in modern abstract algebra. She made her greatest contribution through her work on a general theory of ideals. She worked with David Hilbert and Felix Klein on problems arising from Einstein's theory of relativity. Noether achieved more mathematical eminence than any other woman. Because she cleared the path for women in following years, her life had an importance beyond the development of mathematics.

Quotations:

"In the judgment of the most competent living mathematicians, Fraulein Noether was the most significant creative mathematical genius thus far produced since the higher education of women began."
Albert Einstein
(*New York Times*, May 4, 1935)

Noether is "by far the best woman mathematician of all time, and one of the greatest mathematicians (male or female) of the XXth century."
Jean Dieudonne, 1983
French mathematician

Anecdotes:
Growing up Female

Emmy Noether's childhood was pleasant. She enjoyed playing with her three younger brothers. From the age of seven to 15, she attended "finishing school," where she learned the basic subjects plus household management. She took piano lessons and attended dances. Noether majored in French and English. At 18, she passed the examination by the State of Bavaria to teach at a school for girls.

But Noether really wanted to study mathematics, and she began to think of attending a university for that purpose.

University: For Men Only

At this time in Germany, women were allowed only to audit university courses. With special permission, Noether could listen to lectures, but she could not participate in discussion nor receive credit. She traveled to Göttingen, where she was fortunate to hear some of the great mathematicians of the time. When the University of Erlangen began to admit women, Noether enrolled. She was one of two women among 1000 students. Three years later, in 1907, she received the Ph.D. in mathematics, *summa cum laude*.

Sorry, No Positions Available

Allowing a woman to attend university was one thing; allowing her to teach in one was something else. For many years, Emmy Noether was denied a position in mathematics departments throughout Germany. Even though some of the finest mathematicians spoke on her behalf, tradition and prejudice outweighed her scientific merit.

Noether did get some teaching experience by substituting occasionally for her father, Max. The elder Noether had health problems stemming from a bout with polio when he was 14. When his daughter took over his classes, he relaxed; his students could not have been in better hands.

What's in a Name?

After many years of frustration at not securing a teaching position, Emmy Noether was finally granted a post at the University of Göttingen. She was hired as a *nichtbeamteter ausserordentlicher Professor* ("unofficial professor-extraordinary"). The title was about all she got; there were few responsibilities and there was no salary.

Finally, Some Respect

In 1920, Noether became recognized as an important, innovative force in the development of mathematics. She began to write and publish papers which caught the attention and earned the respect of the finest mathematicians in Europe. Mathematician Herman Weyl said that her work, focusing on abstract rings and the theory of ideals, completely changed the "face of algebra."

Three Strikes You're Out

Just when Noether was getting established in her career, the political scene made life very difficult for her. During the Nazi upheaval in the early 1930s, Noether's appointment and salary were withdrawn and she was forbidden from participation in any academic activity. While some scholars were able to wait out this difficult period, Noether had three strikes against her: 1) she was an intellectual woman, 2) she was Jewish, and 3) she was politically liberal.

Noether faced the situation with courage and grace. As a pacifist, she hoped for a peaceful resolution to the conflict in her country. Finally, however, Noether had no choice but to leave her homeland.

The Land of the Free

In 1933, Emmy Noether was invited to teach at Bryn Mawr College near Philadelphia. Although she spoke in a loud voice with a heavy accent, students quickly became attached to her. She loved to take small groups for Saturday afternoon walks. Sometimes, she became so absorbed in the conversation that she would forget to watch for traffic and the students would have to jump to her rescue. She was a kind, unselfish, and unpretentious woman, sometimes affectionately compared to a "warm loaf of bread."

In the United States, Noether earned her first decent salary. Both her teaching and her research were unusually successful.

Einstein's Colleague

In addition to teaching at Bryn Mawr, Noether was a frequent lecturer at the Institute for Advanced Studies at Princeton. Albert Einstein, who had left Germany under circumstances similar to Noether's, was working at the Institute at that time. He spoke of Noether's contribution to the development of mathematics with highest praise.

A NEW KIND OF ARITHMETIC

Emmy Noether, a great mathematician of the early 1900s, made significant contributions in the area of mathematical systems.

Here is a five-number arithmetic system. Count clockwise around the pentagon and fill in the addition table and the multiplication table for this system.

+	0	1	2	3	4
0					
1					
2				1	
3					
4		0			

×	0	1	2	3	4
0					
1					
2				1	
3					
4			3		

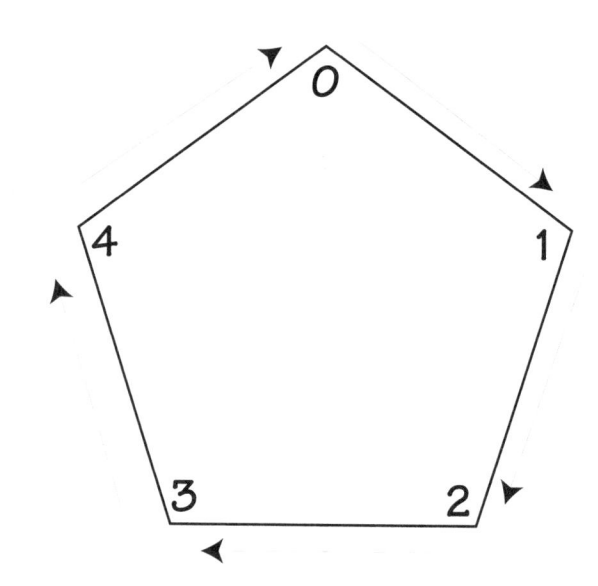

Use your addition and multiplication tables to complete the following.

1. $(4)(2) + (3)(4) =$ _____
2. $3 +$ _____ $= 0$
3. $4(3 + 4) + 1 =$ _____
4. $(2)(3) + (4)(4) + 3 =$ _____
5. $(3)($ _____ $) = 1$
6. $4(3 +$ _____ $) = 1$

ALGEBRA MAGIC

Behind every magic trick is a secret, an explanation of how it's done and why it works. In this trick, the secret is ALGEBRA. Emmy Noether, the great German mathematician, specialized in the study of algebra. With algebra, some of the trickiest tricks can be easily explained.

Study the two examples of this number trick and see what you can discover.

Choose any number	5	8
Add five	5+5=10	8+5=13
Double the result	10X2=20	13X2=26
Subtract four	20-4=16	26-4=22
Divide by two	16/2=8	22/2=11
Subtract the first number	8-5=3	11-8=3
The result?	3	3

Try this number trick with your friends, using different beginning numbers. You will soon discover that 3 is always the answer!

How can you prove that this number trick will always work? Use algebra!

Let X be the number chosen at the beginning of the trick.

Choose any number	X
Add five	X + 5
Double the result	2(X + 5) = 2X + 10
Subtract four	2X + 10 - 4 = 2X + 6
Divide by two	$\frac{(2X + 6)}{2} = X + 3$
Subtract the first number	X + 3 - X = 3
The result?	3

Try making up some number tricks of your own. Do they have an algebraic explanation? Show why they work using algebra!

ALGEBRA SOLVES THE MYSTERY!
A Card Trick to Try

Emmy Noether (1882-1935) used simple algebra to explain many abstract problems. See how algebra solves the mystery in this card trick.

1. Shuffle a standard deck of playing cards.

2. Turn over the top card and place it face up on the table. Use the number on this card as your starting number. Build a stack of cards on this one, adding a card for each number from the starting number until you reach "13." For example, if the number on the starting card is 8, continue counting "9, 10, 11, 12, and 13," placing one card for each number, regardless of what numbers appear on the cards.

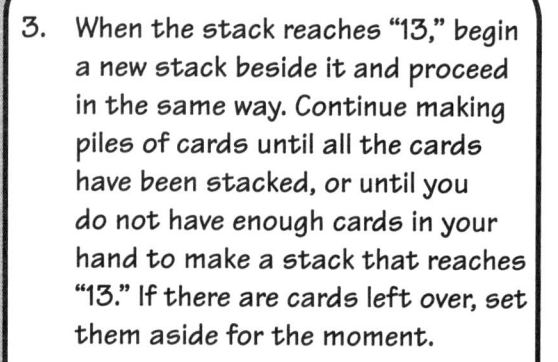

3. When the stack reaches "13," begin a new stack beside it and proceed in the same way. Continue making piles of cards until all the cards have been stacked, or until you do not have enough cards in your hand to make a stack that reaches "13." If there are cards left over, set them aside for the moment.

4. Turn all the stacks over, face down.

5. Choose three stacks at random. Keep them face down on a separate section of the table.

6. Turn over the top card on two of the three stacks.

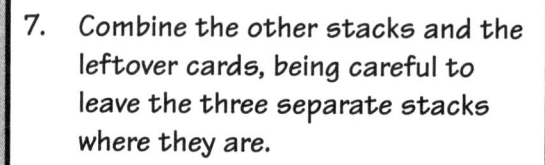

7. Combine the other stacks and the leftover cards, being careful to leave the three separate stacks where they are.

8. Count the cards in your hand.

9. Subtract 10 from the number of cards you hold.

10. From that number, subtract the sum of the numbers on the two cards turned over in step 6.

This number will match the top card of the third overturned stack. Turn over the top card to prove it!

Why does this work? Try using some simple algebra to solve the mystery. Let a, b, and c represent the numbers on the top cards in each of the three stacks set aside in step 5.

Note: For this activity, Ace = 1   Jack = 11   Queen = 12   King = 13

A PUZZLING MYSTERY

Unscramble these Jumbles to form five words that describe the great mathematician Emmy Noether.

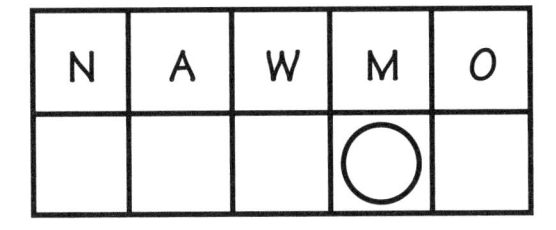

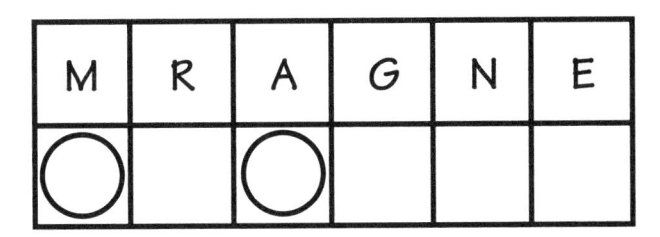

| H | R | A | T | E | C | E |

| N | A | W | M | O |

| M | L | C | A |

| H | R | I | B | G | T |

| M | R | A | G | N | E |

The "mystery" Emmy Noether loved to solve.

Now arrange the circled letters to form the answer to the riddle above.

HISTORICAL CONNECTIONS VOL. III   87   © 2010 AIMS EDUCATION FOUNDATION

Polya
1887 - 1985

GEORGE POLYA
FATHER OF PROBLEM SOLVING

Biographical Facts:

George Polya, 1887-1985, was a Hungarian mathematician. He received his doctorate at the University of Budapest and taught in Vienna and Zurich before emigrating to the United States in 1940. Polya was a friendly, gentle man, much admired for his curiosity and enthusiasm.

Contributions:

Polya is best known for his work in function theory, probability, and applied mathematics. He was especially interested in problem solving, and profoundly influenced the way mathematics is taught. He was a prolific author who wrote more than 250 articles and 10 books.

Quotations by Polya:

"Finished mathematics consists of proofs—mathematics in the making consists of guesses."

"Avoid answering questions that nobody has asked."

"It is better to solve one problem five different ways than to solve five different problems."

"The best way to learn anything is to discover it by yourself."

"I thought I am not good enough for physics and I am too good for philosophy. Mathematics is in between."

Anecdotes:

A Mischievous Child

As a child, George Polya had more energy than he knew how to handle. He loved to walk throughout the city of Budapest, and sometimes "forgot" to tell his mother where he was going. As a teenager, he ran away from home and lived on his own for some time. Polya was an avid soccer player, even after a gash from a teammate's kick required surgery. His short stocky frame helped him win the college prize in wrestling. He was unusually strong; moving furniture was a minor challenge for him.

What's My Line?

Deciding what to study in college was difficult for Polya. During his high school years, he had not enjoyed mathematics. His teachers had emphasized memorization; Polya was more interested in solving problems and making independent discoveries.

He entered the University of Budapest to study law. Soon he switched to biology and then to language and literature. Next he tried philosophy and physics. Largely because of one class he took with a stimulating professor, he finally settled on mathematics.

Dominoes, Anyone?

During his first years of teaching in Zurich, Polya lived in an inexpensive hotel. There he met Mr. Weber, an older gentleman, who invited Polya to play dominoes. One day when Polya arrived for their scheduled match, he was greeted at the door by Mr. Weber's lovely daughter, Stella, who had come to visit. After two years of courtship, Polya and Stella were wed, beginning a 67-year marriage.

A Romantic Walk

Polya never lost his love of walking. In fact, he never drove nor owned an automobile.

One day, a walk through the woods led to an amazing discovery. Polya was somewhat befuddled when he encountered one of his students and his fiancée *three times* in one walk. He was embarrassed, afraid the young lovers would think he was following them. He began to wonder why he kept meeting them in a wood so full of possible paths.

Thinking about this incident led Polya to develop the famous "random walk" problem. In this problem, one imagines a modern city with perfectly square blocks with just as many streets running east and west as north and south. Given any one intersection as the starting point, one could move in any of four directions. If the choice at each intersection were purely random, what is the probability of returning to the starting point? Polya showed that if the walk continues long enough, one is certain to return to the point of origin.

"How to" Solve It

Polya's profound interest in problem solving began when he was hired to work as a tutor for a young boy having trouble with mathematics and science. Polya found that it was very difficult to help his pupil see what to do to solve problems. Finally, after much thought and analysis, he came up with a sketch of the problem-solving process. He set to work to describe this process not just for the boy he was helping, but for all students like him. This led to the writing of one of Polya's most popular and influential books, *How to Solve It*. Printed in at least 17 languages, it has sold over 1,000,000 copies.

Four Simple Steps

In *How to Solve It*, Polya reduced problem solving to four clear steps:

1. Understand the problem.
2. Devise a plan.
3. Carry out the plan.
4. Look back.

Take a Guess

In 1942 Polya began teaching at Stanford University. Students loved his warm, friendly style and his enthusiasm for mathematics. One of his most famous instructions to students who didn't know how to solve a problem was "Guess and Test!" Polya believed that students should use intuition; he encouraged them to experiment and try different approaches to problems. In class, he offered hints and praised every advance his students made.

Teaching Teachers

After he retired, Polya was invited back to Stanford to participate in a series of innovative workshops and courses to help teachers improve their teaching of mathematics. From this experience, he developed his "Ten Commandments for Teachers."*

1. Be interested in your subject.
2. Know your subject.
3. Know about the ways of learning: The best way to learn anything is to discover it by yourself.
4. Try to read the faces of your students, try to see their expectations and difficulties, put yourself in their place.
5. Give them not only information, but "know-how," attitudes of mind, the habit of methodical work.
6. Let them learn guessing.
7. Let them learn proving.
8. Look out for such features of the problem at hand as may be useful in solving the problems to come—try to disclose the general pattern that lies behind the present concrete situation.
9. Do not give away your whole secret at once—let the students guess before you tell it—let them find out by themselves as much as is feasible.
10. Suggest it; do not force it down their throats.

*From Polya, *Mathematical Discovery, Vol. 2*.

April Fools!

Polya had a great sense of humor. In 1946, he and Howard Eves conspired to place an April Fool's problem every year in the April issue of *The American Mathematical Monthly*. They chose "trick" problems that appeared to have complicated, laborious solutions, but were really quite simple. Each year the problem was submitted by the ficticious "Professor Euclide Paracelso Bobasto Umbugio of Guayazuela." Polya and Eves were aghast when readers actually wrote to the magazine requesting Professor Umbugio's home address!

POURING WITH PAILS

George Polya, the great problem solver, loved to pose problems with practical applications. Here is one from his book, *How to Solve It*.

How can you bring up from the river exactly six quarts of water when you have only two containers, a nine quart pail and a four quart pail, to measure with?

Stage 1
9   4

Stage 2
9   4

Stage 3
9   4

Stage 4
9   4

Stage 5
9   4

Stage 6
9   4

Stage 7
9   4

Stage 8
9   4

Use these diagrams to represent 9 and 4 quart pails. Show the stages needed to come up with exactly 6 quarts.

THE LOCKER PROBLEM

George Polya (1887-1985) taught his students to "wish for an easier problem." This problem may seem overwhelming at first, but it can be solved rather easily.

Imagine a high school with 1000 numbered, closed lockers, one for each of its students. Suppose all the students line up and go through the locker area to perform a specific task. Student #1 opens all the lockers. Student #2 closes every even-numbered locker. Student #3 "reverses" every third locker (if open, he closes; if closed, he opens). Each student goes through, reversing the lockers that correspond to his or her position in line. After the 1000th student passes through, which lockers will be open?

Solve this problem by looking at a simpler case. Consider a school with 20 students and 20 lockers. Complete the chart below to discover which lockers will remain open. Use your discovery to solve the original problem.

LOCKER NUMBER

STUDENT	1	2	3	4	5	6	7	8	9	10	11	12	13	14	15	16	17	18	19	20
1	O	O	O	O	O	O	O	O	O	O	O	O	O	O	O	O	O	O	O	O
2	O	C	O	C	O	C	O	C	O	C	O	C	O	C	O	C	O	C	O	C
3	O	C	C	C	O	O	O	C	C	C	O	O	O	C	C	C	O	O	O	C
4	O	C	C	O	O	O	O	O	C	C	O	C	O	C	C	O	O	O	O	O
5																				
6																				
7																				
8																				
9																				
10																				
11																				
12																				
13																				
14																				
15																				
16																				
17																				
18																				
19																				
20																				

FLEA FLIGHT

George Polya (1887-1985), often called "the father of problem solving," liked to show students that problems which looked difficult frequently had simple solutions.

The challenge in this famous dog and flea problem might make you "itch," but the solution is so simple, you can do it in your head.

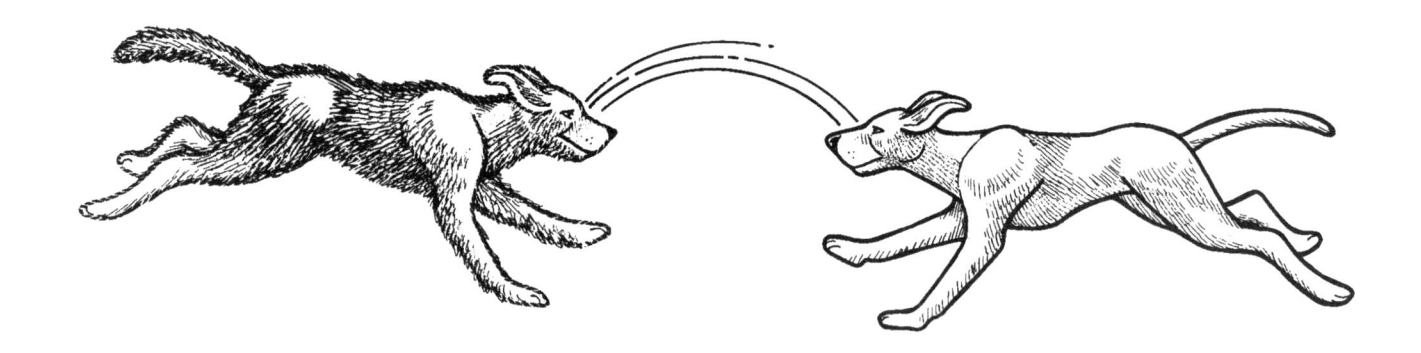

Suppose you have two dogs and one flea. The dogs spy one another from opposite ends of an 100-foot driveway and begin to run towards each other, each at a speed of 10 feet per second.

Starting on one dog, the flea springs back and forth from nose to nose at a speed of 20 feet per second until the dogs collide and flatten him.

How far did the flea travel in all?

BOX IT UP

Suppose you have six squares all the same size. How could you hinge these six squares together so that when the sides are folded up they form a box?

How many unique patterns would result in a box? Draw them on the graph paper below.

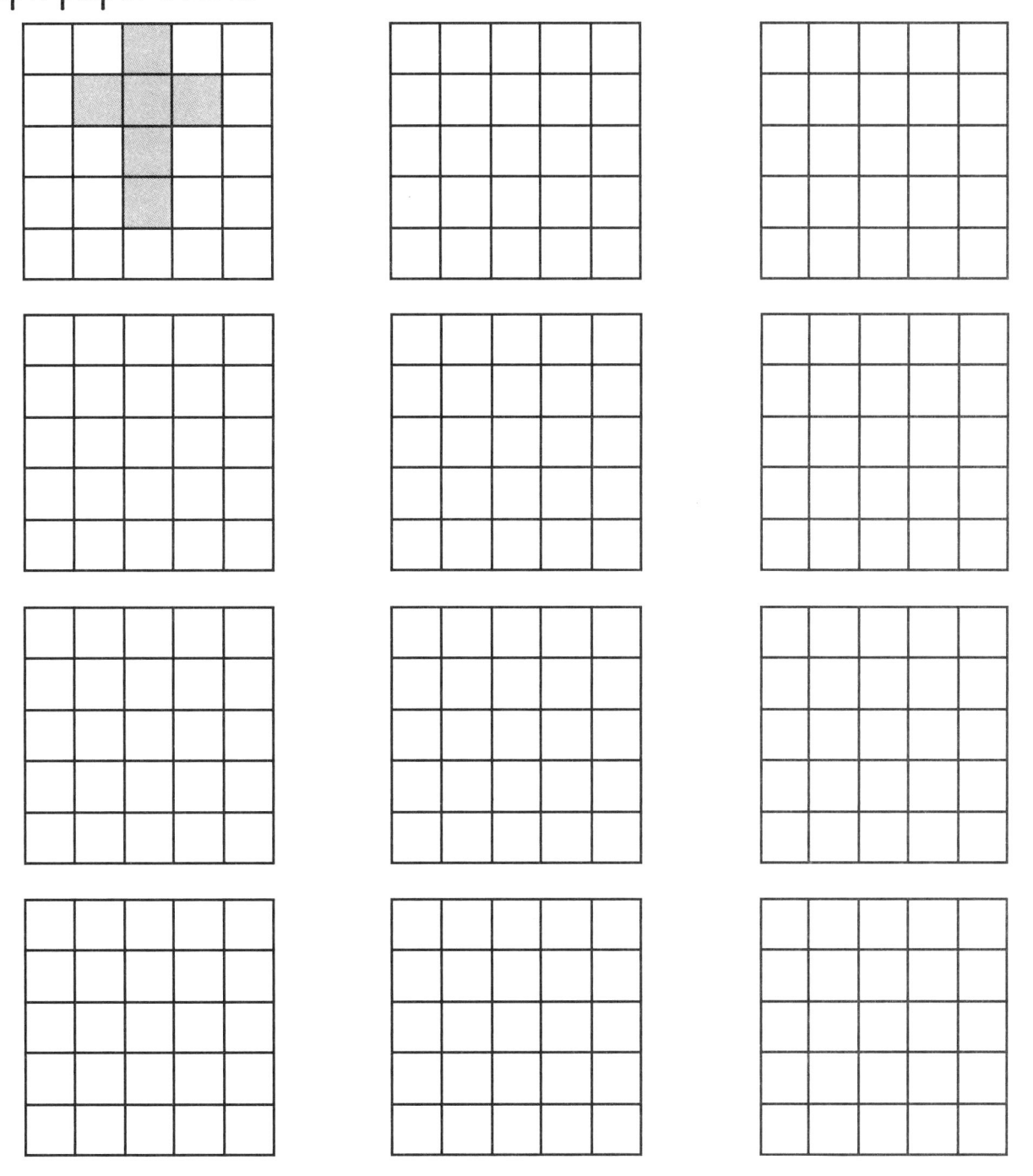

BUILDING BLOCKS

Use any three of the four blocks on the right to create true mathematical sentences. Insert +, -, ×, or ÷ where needed.

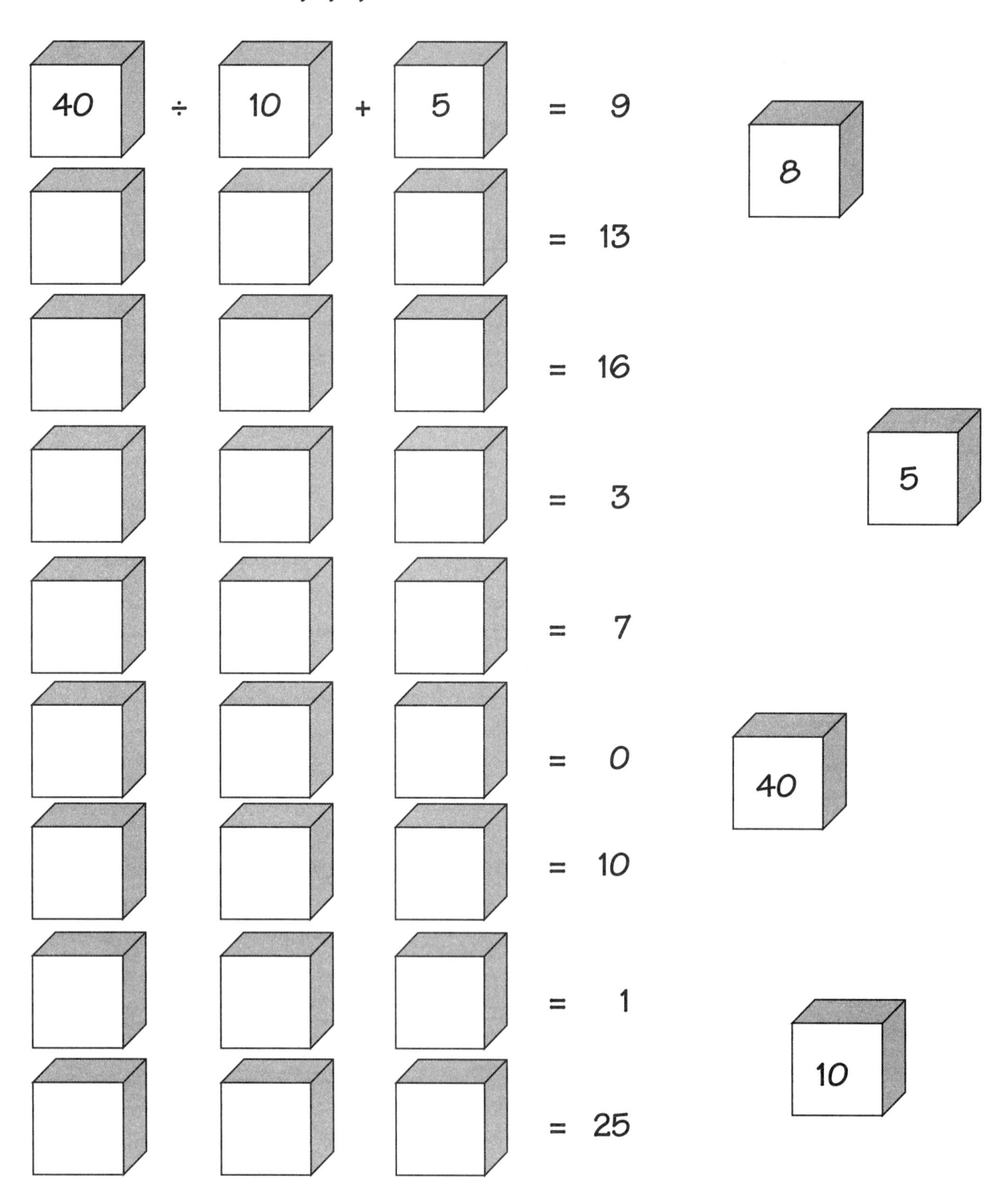

40 ÷ 10 + 5 = 9

= 13

= 16

= 3

= 7

= 0

= 10

= 1

= 25

8

5

40

10

KNIGHT PAIRS ON THE CHESSBOARD

In the game of chess, a knight moves two squares in any direction, then one more square at a right angle.

On an 8 by 8 chessboard we can find many pairs of squares (knight pairs) which are a knight's move apart. For example, on the board shown, squares A and B are a knight's move apart. Two other such pairs are squares B and E and squares C and D.

How many knight pairs are there on an

(a) 8 by 8 chessboard?
(b) n by n chessboard?

Solve this problem by first examining some easier cases. Determine how many knight pairs exist on 3 by 3, 4 by 4, and 5 by 5 boards. The squares are lettered to help you list and count the pairs. Use the pattern that emerges to help you solve the original problem.

3 by 3 Board

4 by 4 Board

5 by 5 Board

Size of Board	Number of Knight Pairs
3 by 3	_____
4 by 4	_____
5 by 5	_____
6 by 6	_____
7 by 7	_____
8 by 8	_____
n by n	_____

APPENDIX

Centimeter Dot Paper

TABLE OF PRIMES

2	233	547	877	1229	1597	1993	2371	2749
3	239	557	881	1231	1601	1997	2377	2753
5	241	563	883	1237	1607	1999	2381	2767
7	251	569	887	1249	1609	2003	2383	2777
11	257	571	907	1259	1613	2011	2389	2789
13	263	577	911	1277	1619	2017	2393	2791
17	269	587	919	1279	1621	2027	2399	2797
19	271	593	929	1283	1627	2029	2411	2801
23	277	599	937	1289	1637	2039	2447	2803
29	281	601	941	1291	1657	2053	2423	2819
31	283	607	947	1297	1663	2063	2437	2833
37	293	613	953	1301	1667	2069	2441	2837
41	307	617	967	1303	1669	2081	2447	2843
43	311	619	971	1307	1693	2083	2459	2851
47	313	631	977	1319	1697	2087	2467	2857
53	317	641	983	1321	1699	2089	2473	2861
59	331	643	991	1327	1709	2099	2477	2879
61	337	647	997	1361	1721	2111	2503	2887
67	347	653	1009	1367	1723	2113	2521	2897
71	349	659	1013	1373	1733	2129	2531	2903
73	353	661	1019	1381	1741	2131	2539	2909
79	359	673	1021	1399	1747	2137	2543	2917
83	367	677	1031	1409	1753	2141	2549	2927
89	373	683	1033	1423	1759	2143	2551	2939
97	379	691	1039	1427	1777	2153	2557	2953
101	383	701	1049	1429	1783	2161	2579	2957
103	389	709	1051	1433	1787	2179	2591	2963
107	397	719	1061	1439	1789	2203	2593	2969
109	401	727	1063	1447	1801	2207	2609	2971
113	409	733	1069	1451	1811	2213	2617	2999
127	419	739	1087	1453	1823	2221	2621	3001
131	421	743	1091	1459	1831	2237	2633	3011
137	431	751	1093	1471	1847	2239	2647	3019
139	433	757	1097	1481	1861	2243	2657	3023
149	439	761	1103	1483	1867	2251	2659	3037
151	443	769	1109	1487	1871	2267	2663	3041
157	449	773	1117	1489	1873	2269	2671	3049
163	457	787	1123	1493	1877	2273	2677	3061
167	461	797	1129	1499	1879	2281	2683	3067
173	463	809	1151	1511	1889	2287	2687	3079
179	467	811	1153	1523	1901	2293	2689	3083
181	479	821	1163	1531	1907	2297	2693	3089
191	487	823	1171	1543	1913	2309	2699	3109
193	491	827	1181	1549	1931	2311	2707	3119
197	499	829	1187	1553	1933	2333	2711	3121
199	503	839	1193	1559	1949	2339	2713	3137
211	509	853	1201	1567	1951	2341	2719	3163
223	521	857	1213	1571	1973	2347	2729	3167
227	523	859	1217	1579	1979	2351	2731	3169
229	541	863	1223	1583	1987	2357	2741	3181

SOME PROGRAMS FOR THE TI-83 GRAPHIC CALCULATOR

PROGRAM: FACTORING

This program will factor into primes any number between 1 and 31,000,000,000. You must input the number to be factored.

FACTOR

```
:Disp "FACTOR PROGRAM"
:Lbl 3
:Disp "Enter Number"
:Input N
:0 → X
:0 → Z
:2 → D
:Goto 1
:Lbl 2
:Z+1 → Z
:If N=1
:Goto 3
:If Z=1
:3 → D
:If Z=1
:Goto 1
:D+2 → D
:If D > √N + 1
:Disp N
:If D > √N + 1
:Goto 3
:Lbl 1
:If N/D ≠ Int(N/D)
:Goto 2
:Disp D
:X+1 → X
:If X/5 = Int(X/5)
:Goto 7
:Lbl 6
:N/D → N
:If N≠1
:Goto 1
:Goto 2
:Lbl 7
:Disp "MORE"
:Pause
:Goto 6
```

PROGRAM: LAGRANGE'S FOUR SQUARE THEOREM

This program will express the inputed number as the sum of four or fewer squares. Note: The calculator may take some time for certain numbers over 1000.

LAGRANGE

```
:Lbl 1
:Disp "INPUT NO."
:Input N
:If √N = int √N
:Then
:√N → I : 0 → K : 0 → Q : 0 → W
:Goto 2
:End
:For (I, int √N, 0, -1)
:For (K, int (√N-I²), 1, -1)
:For (Q, 0, √N)
:For (W, 0, √N)
:I² + K² + Q² + W² → P
:If P = N
:Goto 2
:End :End :End :End
:Goto 3
:Lbl 2
:Disp "SOL FOR N"
:If I ≠ 0 :Disp I²
:If K ≠ 0 :Disp K²
:If Q ≠ 0 :Disp Q²
:If W ≠ 0 :Disp W²
:Lbl 3
:Goto 1
```

PRIME LIST

This program will list all the primes between 1 and the number you enter.
When the display shows MORE simply press the ENTER key to see additional primes.

PRIMES

```
:Input "ENTER NO. ", N
:0 → X
:1 → A
:Disp 2
:Lbl 1
:A + 2 → A
:3 → B
:If A > N
:Stop
:Lbl 3
:If B ≤ √A
:Goto 2
:Disp A
:X + 1 → X
:If (X/5) = int(X/5)
:Then
:Disp "MORE"
:Pause
:End
:Goto 1
:Lbl 2
:If A/B ≤ int(A/B)
:Goto 1
:B + 2 → B
:Goto 3
```

Fibonacci Sequence

This program will list the first 50 terms of the Fibonacci sequence.

FIBSEQ

:1 → X
:0 → Y
:For (N,1,50)
:X + Y → Z
:Disp Z
:Y → X
:Z → Y
:If N/5 = int(N/5)
:Then
:Disp "MORE"
:Pause
:End
:End

Fibonacci Ratio

This program will compute the first 30 consecutive Fibonacci ratios for any Fibonacci-like sequence when the first two terms of the sequence are entered. The ratios always approach the golden ratio which is approximately .618.

FIBRATIO

:Lbl 1
:Input "ENTER A: ",R
:Input "ENTER B: ",S
:R → A :S → B
:For (N,1,30)
:A/B → C
:Disp C
:If N/5 = int(N/5)
:Then
:Disp "MORE"
:Pause
:End
:A + B → D
:B → A
:D → B
:End
:Goto 1

Knight's Pairs

This program will compute the number of pairs of squares which are a knight's move apart for any size board when the size of the board is entered.

KNIGHT

:ClrHome
:Lbl 2
:0→A :0→D :0→E :0→F :0→M
:Input "BOARD SIZE? ",S
:For (R,1,S)
:For (C,1,S)
:If R + 1 > S
:Goto 1
:R → A :C → D :R + 1 → E
:If C - 2 > 0
:Then
:C - 2 → F
:M + 1 → M
:End
:If C + 2 ≤ S
:Then
:C + 2 → F
:M + 1 → M
:End
:If R + 2 < S
:Goto 1
:R → A :C → D :R + 2 → E
:If C - 1 > 0
:Then
:C - 1 → F
:M + 1 → M
:End
:If C + 1 ≤ S
:Then
:C + 1 → F
:M + 1 → M
:End
:Lbl 1
:End
:End
:Disp "NO. KNIGHT PAIRS"
:Disp M
:Goto 2

SUGGESTIONS AND SOLUTIONS

Chapter One: Eratosthenes

The Sieve of Eratosthenes
This activity includes instructions for using Eratosthenes' sieve, a simple but powerful method for finding primes.
Solution:

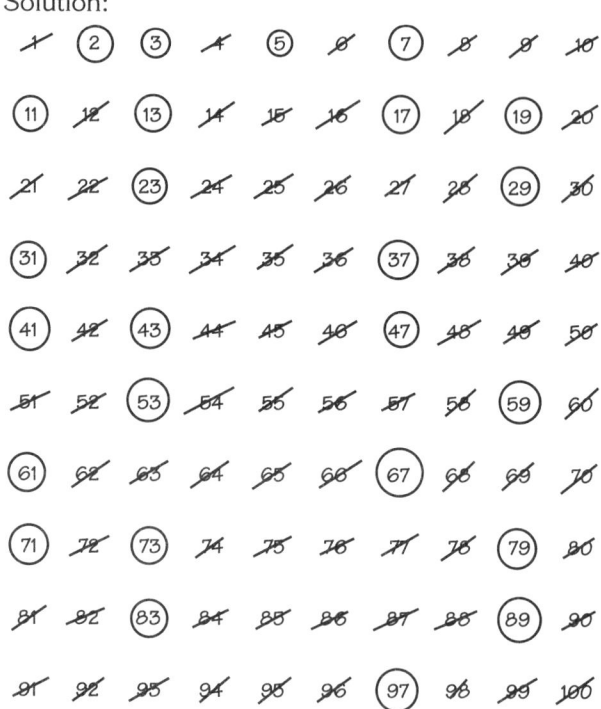

~~1~~ ② ③ ~~4~~ ⑤ ~~6~~ ⑦ ~~8~~ ~~9~~ ~~10~~
⑪ ~~12~~ ⑬ ~~14~~ ~~15~~ ~~16~~ ⑰ ~~18~~ ⑲ ~~20~~
~~21~~ ~~22~~ ㉓ ~~24~~ ~~25~~ ~~26~~ ~~27~~ ~~28~~ ㉙ ~~30~~
㉛ ~~32~~ ~~33~~ ~~34~~ ~~35~~ ~~36~~ ㊲ ~~38~~ ~~39~~ ~~40~~
㊶ ~~42~~ ㊸ ~~44~~ ~~45~~ ~~46~~ ㊼ ~~48~~ ~~49~~ ~~50~~
~~51~~ ~~52~~ ㊳ ~~54~~ ~~55~~ ~~56~~ ~~57~~ ~~58~~ ㊴ ~~60~~
㊶ ~~62~~ ~~63~~ ~~64~~ ~~65~~ ~~66~~ ㊷ ~~68~~ ~~69~~ ~~70~~
㊻ ~~72~~ ㊼ ~~74~~ ~~75~~ ~~76~~ ~~77~~ ~~78~~ ㊽ ~~80~~
~~81~~ ~~82~~ ㊳ ~~84~~ ~~85~~ ~~86~~ ~~87~~ ~~88~~ ㊾ ~~90~~
~~91~~ ~~92~~ ~~93~~ ~~94~~ ~~95~~ ~~96~~ ㊿ ~~98~~ ~~99~~ ~~100~~

Note: a TI-83 program that generates a list of primes appears in the Appendix.

Prime Magic
When students consider the hint offered on this activity sheet, they are prepared to use reasoning and computation to complete the magic squares.
Solution:

47	29	101
113	59	5
17	89	71

157	181	43
13	127	241
211	73	97

109	7	103
67	73	79
43	139	37

277	31	163
43	157	271
151	283	37

107	131	29
11	89	167
149	47	71

83	29	101
89	71	53
41	113	59

Is It Always True?
Solution:
1. 6 = 3 + 3
2. 10 = 3 + 7
3. 14 = 3 + 11
4. 18 = 5 + 13
5. 22 = 5 + 17
6. 24 = 7 + 17
7. 28 = 5 + 23
8. 40 = 3 + 37
9. 64 = 5 + 59
10. 100 = 3 + 9

Remember, there may be more than one way to express some of these numbers as the sum of two primes.

Odds in the Making
Solution:

Odd Number	Prime	Power of two
9	5	4
11	7	4
13	11	2
15	11	4
17	13	4
19	3	16
21	5	16
23	7	16
25	17	8
27	19	8
49	47	2
67	3	64
89	73	16
119	103	16
131	3	128

The Earth and the Wire Belt
This activity leads students through a problem-solving activity with a surprising result. Encourage students to perform the computation themselves to confirm the answer.

The radius of the Earth has no effect on the answer to this problem.

HISTORICAL CONNECTIONS VOL. III

Chapter Two: Fibonacci

Fibonacci Discoveries

The activity entitled "Fibonacci Discoveries" encourages students to discover several of the many patterns in the Fibonacci sequence.
Solution:
1, 1, 2, 3, 5, 8, 13, 21, 34, 55, 89, 144, <u>233</u>, <u>377</u>, <u>610</u>,

Fibonacci Number	2	3	5	8	13	21	34	55
Square of Number	4	9	25	64	169	441	1156	3025
Product of Numbers Before and After	3	10	24	65	168	442	1155	3026
Difference	1	1	1	1	1	1	1	1

$1^2 = 1 \times 1$
$1^2 + 1^2 = 1 \times 2$
$1^2 + 1^2 + 2^2 = 2 \times 3$
$1^2 + 1^2 + 2^2 + 3^2 = 3 \times 5$
$1^2 + 1^2 + 2^2 + 3^2 + 5^2 = \underline{5} \times \underline{8}$
$1^2 + 1^2 + 2^2 + 3^2 + 5^2 + 8^2 = \underline{8} \times \underline{13}$

$1^2 + 1^2 + 2^2 + 3^2 + 5^2 + 8^2 + 13^2 = \underline{13} \times \underline{21}$

Note: a TI-83 program that lists terms of the Fibonacci sequence appears in the Appendix.

Does 64 = 65?

While this problem appears paradoxical, careful cutting and repositioning of the pieces should reveal an imperfect fit. The overlap or space between pieces will equal one unit. This is shown in the earlier discovery that the products of the two numbers preceding and following a Fibonacci number is either one less or one more than the square of the Fibonacci number.
Other possible shapes and areas:

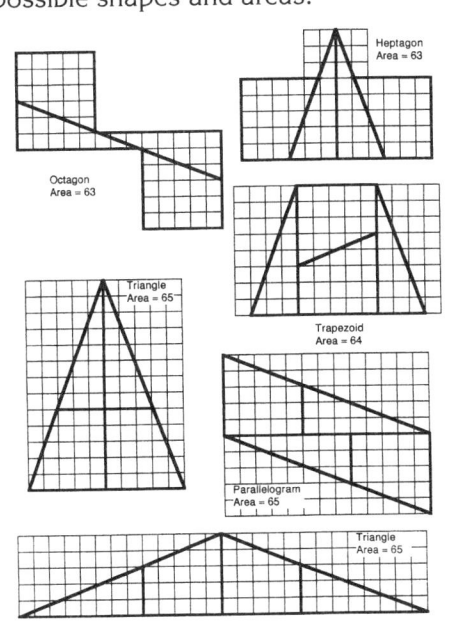

Octagon Area = 63
Heptagon Area = 63
Triangle Area = 65
Trapezoid Area = 64
Parallelogram Area = 65
Triangle Area = 65

The Path from Pisa
Solution:

Dimensions	Number of Arrangements
2 by 1	1
2 by 2	2
2 by 3	3
2 by 4	5
2 by 5	8
2 by 6	13
2 by 7	21
2 by 8	34
2 by 9	55
2 by 10	89

The pattern in the table reflects the Fibonacci sequence.

Fibonacci Magic

Students may use algebra to show that the sum of the numbers above the line will always be the second number below the line minus the second number from the beginning.

Suppose the first two terms of a Fibonacci-like sequence are a and b. As an example, make a list of terms and draw a line under 5a+8b.

Note that the second number below the line is 13a + 21b. When the second term in the list, b, is subtracted, the answer is 13a + 20b, the sum of the numbers above the line.

a
b
a+b
a+2b
2a+3b
3a+5b
<u>5a+8b</u>
8a+13b
13a+21b

More Fibonacci Magic

Some simple algebra will show that the sum of ten terms in a Fibonacci-like sequence is always the seventh term.

Let a and b be the first two terms of a Fibonacci-like sequence. The first ten terms are as follows.

a
b
a+b
a+2b
2a+3b

HISTORICAL CONNECTIONS VOL. III

3a+5b
5a+8b
8a+13b
13a+21b
21a+34b

Notice that the sum of these ten terms is 11 times the seventh term, namely 11(5a+8b) = 55a +88b.

Fibonacci's Golden Ratios
Solution

Fibonacci Ratio	Expressed to Three Decimal Places
$\frac{1}{1}$	1.000
$\frac{1}{2}$	.500
$\frac{2}{3}$	.667
$\frac{3}{5}$	.600
$\frac{5}{8}$	.625
$\frac{8}{13}$	.615
$\frac{13}{21}$	.619
$\frac{21}{34}$	.618
$\frac{34}{55}$	.618
$\frac{55}{89}$	.618

The ratios are approaching the golden ratio, which is approximately .618. Any Fibonacci-like sequence will produce ratios that approach this number. A golden rectangle is a rectangle where the ratio of the width to the length is approximately .618.
Note: a TI-83 program that computes Fibonacci ratios appears in the Appendix.

On the Road to Rome
Solution:

```
        7 women
       49 mules
      343 sacks
     2401 loaves
    16807 knives
   117649 sheaths
  137, 256 total number on the way to Rome
```

Chapter Three: Descartes

Plot and Swat
Solution:

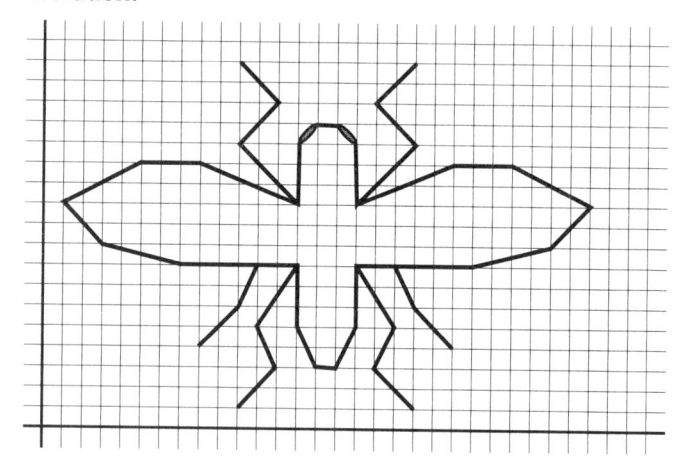

On a Roll
Students should enjoy playing this game, which will give them practice at plotting coordinates.

Area The Easy Way
This activity illustrates the power Descartes' analytic geometry brings to certain problem situations. Aerial surveyors often use the method described on the activity sheet to find areas of irregular shaped regions.
Solution:
1. 42 square units
2. 23 square units
3. 44 square units

Descartes' Word Search
Solution:

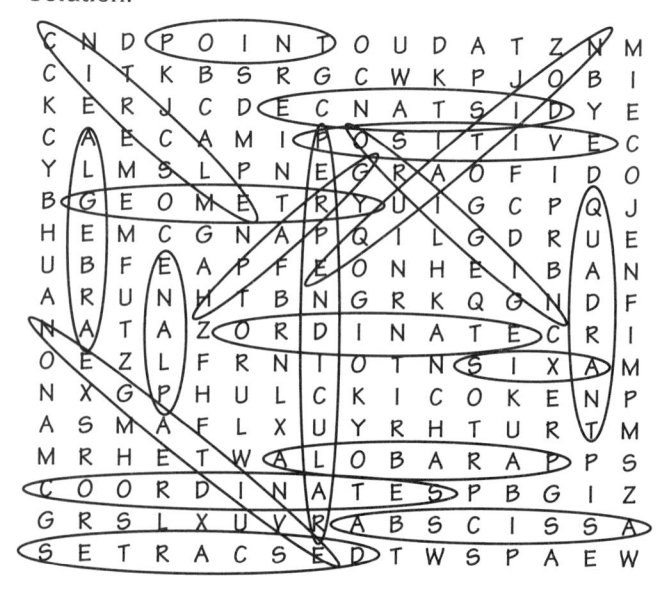

The Best Put to Test: A Skit to Read
Assign parts to students and allow them to read the skit aloud to learn about Descartes.

Chapter Four: Agnesi

The Witch of Agnesi
This activity asks students to graph the curve studied by Maria Agnesi.
Solution:

X	Y
-8	.8
-7	1.0
-6	1.2
-5	1.6
-4	2
-3	2.6
-2	3.2
-1	3.8
0	4
1	3.8
2	3.2
3	2.6
4	2
5	1.6
6	1.2
7	1.0
8	.8

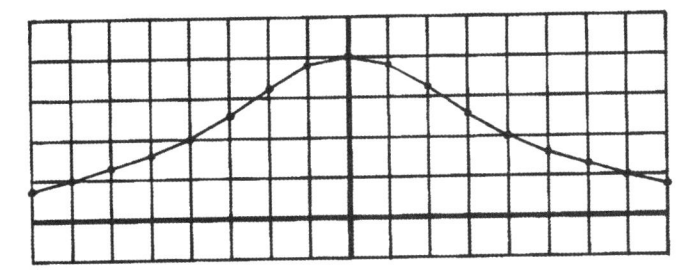

1. When X is 50, Y is approximately .025.
2. The curve will never cross the X-axis because for all values of X, Y is a positive number.

Exploring Isoperimetric Figures
Students may cut out large isoperimetric figures and arrange them on a bulletin board to help visualize the differences in areas.

Solution:
Areas of isoperimetric figures arranged from largest area to smallest:

Figure	Area
Circle	412 sq ft
Square	324 sq ft
Rectangle (12,24)	288 sq ft
Rectangle (10,26)	260 sq ft
Equilateral triangle	250 sq ft
Isosceles triangle	240 sq ft
Hexagon	236 sq ft
Right triangle	216 sq ft

X's, Y's, and Zzzzz's: A Skit to Read
Assign parts to students and read this skit in class to stimulate interest in Maria Agnesi's life.

Maria's Puzzle
Tell students the story of Agnesi's life or read "The Gift of Simplicity" from *Mathematicians Are People, Too, Volume 2* in preparation for doing this puzzle. Some teachers may wish to provide a list of answer words.
Solution:

Chapter Five: Lagrange

Lagrange's Four Square Theorem
This activity asks students to verify the theorem for a number of cases. Encourage students to watch for emerging patterns as they complete the activity.

Solution:
More than one representation is often possible. Only one is given.
1 = 1
2 = 1+1
3 = 1+1+1
4 = 4
5 = 4 + 1
6 = 4 + 1 + 1
7 = 4 + 1 + 1 + 1
8 = 4 + 4
9 = 9

10 = 9 + 1
11 = 9 + 1 + 1
12 = 9 + 1 + 1 + 1
13 = 9 + 4
14 = 9 + 4 + 1
15 = 9 + 4 + 1 + 1
16 = 16
17 = 16 + 1
18 = 16 + 1 + 1
19 = 16 + 1 + 1 + 1
20 = 16 + 4
21 = 16 + 4 + 1
22 = 16 + 4 + 1 + 1
23 = 9 + 9 + 4 + 1
24 = 16 + 4 + 4
25 = 25
26 = 25 + 1
27 = 25 + 1 + 1
28 = 25 + 1 + 1 + 1
29 = 25 + 4
30 = 25 + 4 + 1
48 = 36 + 4 + 4 + 4
56 = 36 + 16 + 4
77 = 64 + 9 + 4
87 = 81 + 4 + 1 + 1
92 = 81 + 9 + 1 + 1
114 = 100 + 9 + 4 + 1

1. Of the integers from 10 to 20, all but 11, 14, and 15 have more than one representation.
2. Of the integers from 1 to 20 only 7 and 15 cannot be expressed as the sum of three or fewer squares.

Note: a TI-83 program related to this activity appears in the Appendix.

Predictable Products

Multiply 4 Consecutive Numbers	Product	Product Plus 1	Written as a Square
1 × 2 × 3 × 4	24	25	5^2
2 × 3 × 4 × 5	120	121	11^2
3 × 4 × 5 × 6	360	361	19^2
4 × 5 × 6 × 7	840	841	29^2
5 × 6 × 7 × 8	1680	1681	41^2
6 × 7 × 8 × 9	3024	3025	55^2
7 × 8 × 9 × 10	5040	5041	71^2
30 × 31 × 32 × 33			991^2
50 × 51 × 52 × 53			2651^2
n(n + 1)(n + 2)(n + 3)			$[n(n + 3) + 1]^2$

Help students discover that the product of the first and fourth numbers in each row of 4 consecutive numbers can be used to determine the number in the last column of the table. For example, in the row with 3 × 4 × 5 × 6, multiply 3 times 6, add 1, and square, obtaining 19^2.

In general, $n(n + 1)(n + 2)(n + 3) + 1$ can be shown to be equal to $[n(n + 3) + 1]^2$. Students with algebra background can be asked to multiply these out to show they are equal.

The Metric Highway
Solution:

Miles	Kilometers
10	10 + 5 + 1 = 16
20	20 + 10 + 2 = 32
30	30 + 15 + 3 = 48
40	40 + 20 + 4 = 64
50	50 + 25 + 5 = 80
60	60 + 30 + 6 = 96
70	70 + 35 + 7 = 112
80	80 + 40 + 8 = 128
90	90 + 45 + 9 = 144
100	100 + 50 + 10 = 160
200	200 + 100 + 20 = 320
n	$n + \frac{1}{2}n + \frac{1}{10}n = 1.6n$

Metric Crossword
Lagrange played a key role in the adoption of the metric system in Europe, and is often called the "Father of the Metric System." This puzzle may be difficult for students if they are unfamiliar with metric terms. Provide conversion tables to help them.

Metric Mania

This activity may challenge students who are unfamiliar with the metric system. Teachers may wish to provide conversion tables for student reference.

Solution:
1. a
2. a
3. b
4. c
5. b
6. c
7. b
8. c
9. b
10. c
11. b
12. c

Chapter Six: Somerville

Just Passing Through

If necessary, remind students how to find the greatest common divisor. Note that a diagonal must intersect a square at more than one point to be "passing through."

Solution:

LENGTH L	WIDTH W	GCD OF L AND W	NO. OF UNIT SQUARES
3	2	1	4
3	1	1	3
4	2	2	4
5	3	1	7
6	4	2	8
6	3	3	6
7	5	1	11
Use your rule to answer the rest.			
100	75	25	150
600	50	50	600
300	200	100	400

The rule is L + W - GCD = No. of unit squares.

Star Shapes

Solution:
The formula, $A = \frac{1}{2}B + I - 1$, yields the following solutions:

1. $\frac{1}{2}(10) + 1 - 1 = 5$
2. $\frac{1}{2}(6) + 1 - 1 = 3$
3. $\frac{1}{2}(4) + 2 - 1 = 3$
4. $\frac{1}{2}(8) + 3 - 1 = 6$
5. $\frac{1}{2}(11) + 0 - 1 = 4\frac{1}{2}$
6. $\frac{1}{2}(17) + 1 - 1 = 8\frac{1}{2}$

Where Does the Ocean End?

This problem is an application of the Pythagorean theorem with a surprising result. It is the kind of problem that interested Mary Somerville.

Students should use a calculator to complete these exercises. Some may need to be reminded that 1 mile = 5280 feet and that in the equation each term represents miles.

Solution:
A person six feet tall would be able to see 3.02 miles of ocean.
$x^2 + 4000^2 = (4000 + \frac{6}{5280})^2$
$x^2 = 9.09$
$x = 3.02$ miles

Exercises:
1. $x^2 + 4000^2 = (4000 + \frac{4}{5280})^2$
   $x^2 = 6.06$
   $x = 2.46$ miles
2. $x^2 + 4000^2 = (4000 + \frac{20}{5280})^2$
   $x^2 = 30.30$
   $x = 5.50$ miles
3. $x^2 + 4000^2 = (4000 + \frac{100}{5280})^2$
   $x^2 = 151.52$
   $x = 12.31$ miles

An Ant Thermometer

Solution:

Temperature (Celsius)	Speed of Ants in Cm/Minute
13	8
14	16
15	24
16	32
17	40
18	48
19	56
n	8n - 96

Chapter Seven: Dodgson

Dodgson's Doublets
A helpful problem solving strategy for this activity is to work backwards as well as forwards.
Solution:
Here are possible solutions, not necessarily the shortest.

1. SIX	2. EAST	3. BOAT	4. MEAN
SIN	PAST	COAT	BEAN
TIN	PEST	COST	BEAD
TEN	WEST	CAST	BEND
		CASE	BIND
		CAKE	KIND
		LAKE	

5. ADD	6. SNOW	7. HATE
AID	SLOW	HAVE
AIM	SLOT	HIVE
HIM	SOOT	LIVE
HUM	BOOT	LOVE
SUM	BOLT	
	BELT	
	BELL	
	BALL	

Dodgson's Discovery
There is more to this activity then first meets the eye. Encourage students to watch for patterns.

Help students discover that if a^2 and b^2 are the squares in the first two columns respectively, then the two squares required in the last column are $(a + b)^2$ and $(a - b)^2$.

An appropriate hint might be to ask students how the square root of the numbers in the first two columns might lead to the results in the last column.

A little algebra shows that this always works.
$(a + b)^2 + (a - b)^2 = a^2 + 2ab + b^2 + a^2 - 2ab + b^2 = 2a^2 + 2b^2 = 2(a^2 + b^2)$

Double the sum of two squares can always be expressed as the sum of two squares.

First Square	Second Square	Sum of Squares Chosen	Double of Sum	Expressed as Sum of Two Squares
4	9	13	26	1 + 25
25	64	89	178	9 + 169
4	16	20	40	4 + 36
9	25	34	68	4 + 64
16	25	41	82	1 + 81
36	49	85	170	1 + 169
64	81	145	290	1 + 289
4	36	40	80	16 + 64
16	100	116	232	36 + 196
64	121	185	370	9 + 361

Lighthearted Logic
To help students reach the correct conclusion using all ten statements, arrange them as follows:

3. If I don't avoid an animal, then I don't detest them.
9. If I don't detest them, then animals take to me.
6. If an animal takes to me, then it is in this house.
1. If an animal is in this house, then it is a cat.
5. If an animal is a cat, then it kills mice.
8. If an animal kills mice, then it is carnivora.
4. If an animal is carnivorous, then it prowls at night.
10. If an animal prowls at night, then it loves to gaze at the moon.
2. If an animal loves to gaze at the moon, then it is suitable for a pet.
7. If an animal is suitable for a pet, then it is not a kangaroo.

Solution:
If I don't avoid an animal, then it is not a kangaroo.

More Logic Puzzles
To reach the correct conclusion using all ten statements arrange them as follows:

5. If it is raining, then I stay home.
3. If I stay home, then I study.
6. If I study, then I get good grades.
1. If I get good grades, then I go to college.
4. If I go to college, then I get a good job.
2. If I get a good job, then I make a good salary.

Soluton: If it is raining, then I make a good salary.

4. If it freezes in September, then the pears do not grow.
3. If the pears are not growing, then the children are wearing old shoes.
1. If they wear old shoes, then the children wear holes in their socks.
5. If the children are wearing holes in their socks, then the sock business is booming.
2. If the sock business booms, then Joe can buy a new car.
7. If Joe has a new car, then Joe has dates quite often.
6. If Joe has dates quite often, then all the young ladies are happy.

Solution: If it freezes in September, then the young ladies are happy.

The Real Alice: A Skit to Read
Students may be surprised to learn that a mathematician wrote *Alice's Adventures in Wonderland*. Invite them to take turns reading the parts in this short skit that reveal some of Dodgson's personality and trace the true source of his best-known story.

Chapter Eight: Venn

Problem Solving Using Venn Diagrams
This activity introduces students to the dynamic problem-solving power of Venn diagrams. After completing the activity, students may be encouraged to design some Venn diagram problems on their own.

Students are often helped by the suggestion that they start in the center of the diagram, first filling in the region that reflects the most overlap.

Solution to Problem 1:

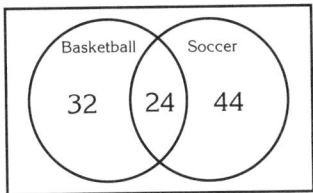

Basketball: 32, Overlap: 24, Soccer: 44

Solution to Problem 2:

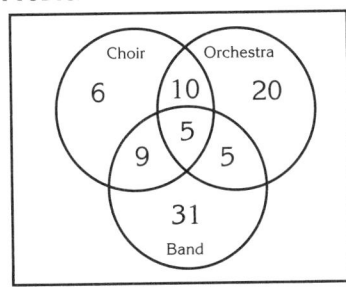

Choir: 6, Choir∩Orchestra: 10, Orchestra: 20, Center (all three): 5, Choir∩Band: 9, Orchestra∩Band: 5, Band: 31

Venn Diagrams Solve the Problem
Solution to Problem 1:

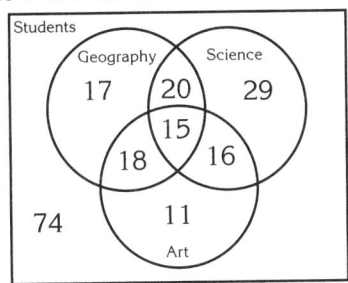

Students; Geography: 17, Geography∩Science: 20, Science: 29, Center: 15, Geography∩Art: 18, Science∩Art: 16, Art: 11, Outside: 74

Problem 2:

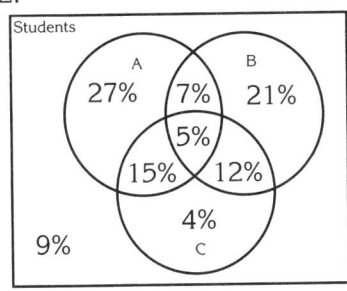

Students; A: 27%, A∩B: 7%, B: 21%, Center: 5%, A∩C: 15%, B∩C: 12%, C: 4%, Outside: 9%

Who's in Charge?
Solution:
The manager is Mary.
The assistant manager is John.
The cashier is Susan.
The secretary is Fred.
The clerk is Adam.
The computer programmer is Sam.

Crossing the River
Solution:
The showman must first take the goat across. He comes back alone and takes the wolf across and brings the goat back. Next he takes the cabbage across and finally returns to collect the goat.

Rowing Relay
Solution:
Problem 1: Yellow team
The minimum time is 55 minutes.
Here are two solutions:

A and D go over	20 minutes
D comes back	5 minutes
B and D go over	15 minutes
D comes back	5 minutes
C and D go over	10 minutes
Total Time	55 minutes

C and D go over	10 minutes
D comes back	5 minutes
A and B go over	20 minutes
C comes back	10 minutes
C and D go over	10 minutes
Total Time	55 minutes

Problem 2: Red team

C and D go over	10 minutes
D comes back	5 minutes
A and B go over	25 minutes
C comes back	10 minutes
C and D go over	10 minutes
Total Time	60 minutes

Chapter Nine: Noether

A New Kind of Arithmetic
Solution:

+	0	1	2	3	4
0	0	1	2	3	4
1	1	2	3	4	0
2	2	3	4	0	1
3	3	4	0	1	2
4	4	0	1	2	3

Remember, multiplication may be understood as repeated addition.

X	0	1	2	3	4
0	0	0	0	0	0
1	0	1	2	3	4
2	0	2	4	1	3
3	0	3	1	4	2
4	0	4	3	2	1

1. 0
2. 2
3. 4
4. 0
5. 2
6. 1

Algebra Magic
Students are usually fascinated by number tricks. This one demonstrates the power of algebra to show why it works.

Algebra Solves the Mystery
This activity features a card trick that seems complex, but may be performed and understood by students with the help of algebra.
Solution:
Number of cards in stack with "a" on top: 14 - a
Number of cards in stack with "b" on top: 14 - b
Number of cards in stack with "c" on top: 14 - c
Number of cards in "left-over" stack: 52 - (14-a) - (14 - b) - (14 - c) = 10 + a + b + c
When 10 cards are removed from the "left-over" stack, a+b+c cards remain. After removing, for example, "a" cards and "c" cards, "b" cards are left (a+b+c-a-c=b). "b" equals the top number of the third stack of cards!

A Puzzling Mystery
Solution:

H	R	A	T	E	C	E
T	E	(A)	C	H	(E)	R

N	A	W	M	O
W	O	M	(A)	N

M	L	C	A
C	A	(L)	M

H	R	I	B	G	T
(B)	R	I	G	H	T

M	R	A	G	N	E
(G)	E	(R)	M	A	N

A	L	G	E	B	R	A

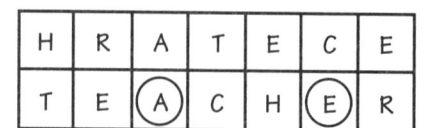

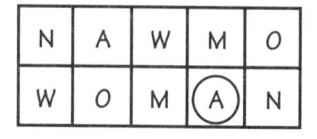

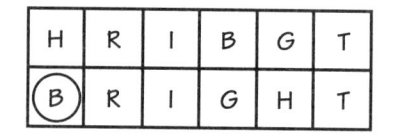

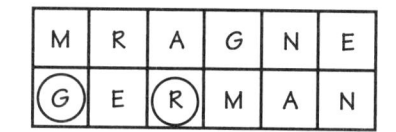

Chapter Ten: Polya

Pouring with Pails
This activity features a problem from Polya's *How to Solve It*. Discuss approaches to this problem to get students started. If appropriate, consider bringing containers and water into the classroom and allow students to experiment.
Solution:

Stage 1: The 9 qt pail is full and the 4 qt pail is empty.

Stage 2: The 4 qt pail is filled from the 9 qt pail, leaving 5 qts in the 9 qt pail.

Stage 3: Discard water in the 4 qt pail.

Stage 4: The 4 qt pail is filled again from the 9 qt pail, leaving 1 qt in the 9 qt pail.

Stage 5: Discard water in the 4 qt pail.

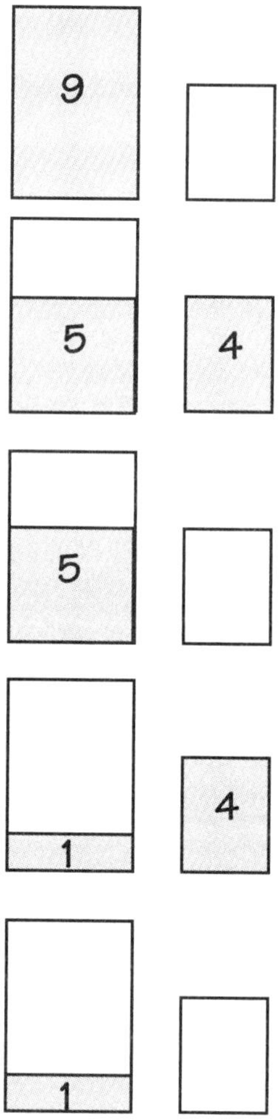

Stage 6: Pour the 1 qt of water from the 9 qt pail into the 4 qt pail.

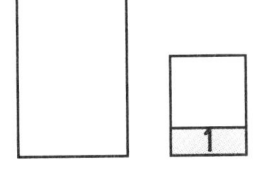

Stage 7: Fill the 9 qt pail with water from the river.

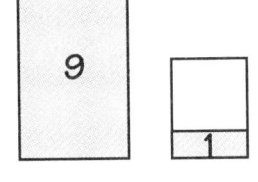

Stage 8: Fill the 4 qt pail from the 9 qt pail, leaving the desired 6 qts in the 9 qt pail.

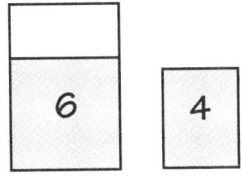

Suggestion: Other problems like this one may be created by changing the size of the containers and/or the amount of water to be collected.

The Locker Problem
The introduction of this activity often evokes groans and gasps, but students soon recognize the power in Pólya's suggestion of solving an easier problem first.
Solution:
In a school with 20 lockers and 20 students, the lockers open after all 20 students have passed through are 1, 4, 9, and 16—the perfect squares!

In the school with 1000 lockers and students, the lockers remaining open after the 1000th student has gone through are the perfect squares: 1, 4, 9, 16, 25, 36, 49, 64, 81, 100, 121, 144, 169, 196, 225, 256, 289, 324, 361, 400, 441, 484, 529, 576, 625, 676, 729, 784, 841, 900, and 961.

Flea Flight
Solution:
The key to mentally solving this problem is to recognize that the dogs are approaching each other at a rate of 20 ft/sec. (10 ft/sec for each dog). Since the driveway is 100 ft long, they will run towards each other for 5 seconds (100ft/20 ft/sec = 5 seconds). During these 5 seconds, the flea is flying at a constant speed of 20 ft/sec. Therefore, the flea will fly a total of 100 feet, the answer to the problem.

Box Making
Students may cut out shapes and fold them into boxes. These may be mounted on a bulletin board to show the collected options. There are eleven unique solutions, none of which is congruent.
Solution:

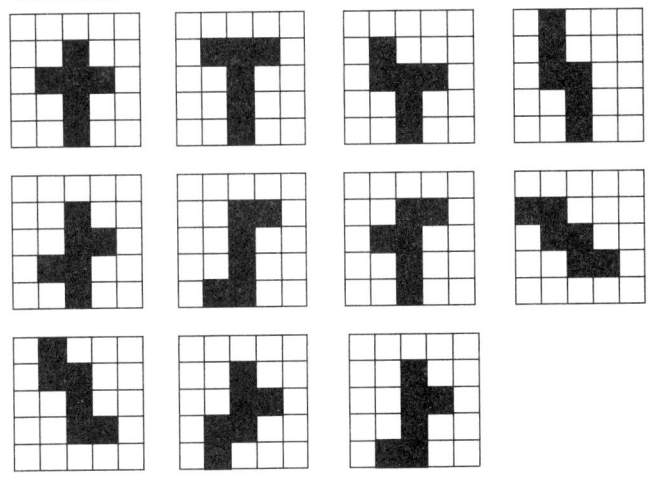

Building Boxes
Students may use their creativity to design problems in a variety of ways.
Possible solutions:
$40 \div 10 + 5 = 9$
$10 + 8 - 5 = 13$
$10 \div 5 \times 8 = 16$
$5 + 8 - 10 = 3$
$10 - 8 + 5 = 7$
$5 \times 8 - 40 = 0$
$10 \div 5 + 8 = 10$
$5 - 40 \div 10 = 1$
$40 - 10 - 5 = 25$

Knight Pairs on the Chessboard
Encourage students to be orderly in listing the knight pairs. For the 3 by 3 board the list might look like this:
A and H
A and F
B and G
B and I
C and D
C and H
D and I
F and G

HISTORICAL CONNECTIONS VOL. III © 2010 AIMS Education Foundation

Once the data have been collected for the 3 by 3, 4 by 4, and 5 by 5 boards, look for a pattern. Dividing the numbers in the second column results in the triangular numbers. This can be used to find the general formula.

Note: a TI-83 program for this activity appears in the Appendix. Some teachers may wish to show how technology can be used to collect data for problems such as this.

Solution:

Size of Board	Number of Knight Pairs
3 by 3	8
4 by 4	24
5 by 5	48
6 by 6	80
7 by 7	120
8 by 8	168
n by n	$4n^2 - 12n + 8$

RESOURCES FOR LIBRARY AND CLASSROOM

Abbott, David
THE BIOGRAPHICAL DICTIONARY OF SCIENTISTS: MATHEMATICIANS
New York: Peter Bedrick Books, 1986
   This is an authoritative and accessible reference work. Includes a chronological introduction and alphabetical arrangement of entries, plus a useful glossary.

Alic, Margaret
HYPATIA'S HERITAGE
London: The Women's Press, 1990.
   Biographical and scientific information on the lives and times of outstanding women scientists and mathematicians from antiquity to the late 19th century.

Beckman, Petr
A HISTORY OF PI
New York: St. Martin's Press, 1971
   Readable, interesting source that reveals the background of the times and the personalities associated with the development of pi.

Bell, E.T.
MEN OF MATHEMATICS
New York: Simon & Schuster, 1965
   The classic work in mathematics history. Includes lots of detail and useful information.

Dunham, William
JOURNEY THROUGH GENIUS: THE GREAT THEOREMS OF MATHEMATICS
New York: John Wiley & Sons, Inc., 1990
   This work explores some of the most significant and enduring ideas in mathematics, emphasizing the humanity of the great mathematicians.

Eves, Howard W.
AN INTRODUCTION TO THE HISTORY OF MATHEMATICS
Fifth Edition
New York: Saunders College Publishing, 1983
   A popular text for history of math classes. Eves traces the development of mathematics with good humor and informative detail.

Eves, Howard W.
IN MATHEMATICAL CIRCLES (VOL 1 & 2)
Boston: Prindle, Weber & Schmidt, Inc., 1969
   These popular books contain chronologically arranged anecdotes about mathematicians and their discoveries. Delightful, short bits of information that are useful and understandable.

Grinstein, Louise and Paul Campbell
WOMEN OF MATHEMATICS: A BIBLIOGRAPHIC SOURCEBOOK
New York: Greenwood Press, 1987.
   Contains brief biographies of 43 women mathematicians, plus comments on their work and useful bibliographic sources.

Hollingdale, Stuart
MAKERS OF MATHEMATICS
London: Penguin Books, 1989
   Chapters on mathematicians from Pythagoras to Einstein provide useful biographical information, accompanied by a solid review of the mathematics these persons worked with.

Katz, Victor
A HISTORY OF MATHEMATICS
New York, New York: HarperCollins, 1993
   A readable college text, filled with useful information and illustrations.

Mitchell, Merle
MATHEMATICAL HISTORY: ACTIVITIES, PUZZLES, STORIES, AND GAMES
Reston, Virginia: National Council of Teachers of Mathematics, 1978
   This is a collection of enrichment resources for use in the upper elementary grades. Activities may be photocopied for classroom use.

MULTICULTURALISM IN MATHEMATICS, SCIENCE, AND TECHNOLOGY: READINGS AND ACTIVITIES
Menlo Park, CA: Addison-Wesley, 1993
   A source book for teachers, including representation from a wide range of cultural groups. Black line masters may be reproduced for classroom use.

National Council of Teachers of Mathematics
HISTORICAL TOPICS FOR THE MATHEMATICS CLASSROOM
Reston, Virginia: NCTM, 1989
   This work, first commissioned in 1969, is designed to help teachers teach mathematics from a historical perspective. It is divided into chapters on the history of numbers, the history of geometry, the history of algebra, etc., and includes a useful list of resources.

Pappas, Theoni
THE JOY OF MATHEMATICS
San Carlos, CA: Wide World Publishing/Tetra, 1989
   This book unveils the inseparable relationship of mathematics to the world in which we live. In one or two page "glimpses," the reader enjoys games, puzzles, interesting facts, and historic background.

Pappas, Theoni
MORE JOY OF MATHEMATICS
San Carlos, CA: Wide World Publishing/Tetra, 1991
   Like Pappas' first book, this collection also provides brief but fascinating information on how mathematics can be seen in nature, science, music, architecture, literature, and history.

Perl, Teri
MATH EQUALS—BIOGRAPHIES OF WOMEN MATHEMATICIANS
Menlo Park, CA: Addison-Wesley, 1978
   This is a readable collection of resources on the lives and work of nine women, including activities which relate to their work.

Reimer, Luetta and Wilbert Reimer
MATHEMATICIANS ARE PEOPLE, TOO, Volumes 1 and 2
Palo Alto, CA: Dale Seymour Publications, 1990, 1995
    These collections of illustrated stories dramatically recreate episodes from the lives of 30 great mathematicians, including seven women. For students to read or for teachers to read aloud, the books highlight the human element in mathematics. Appropriate for students in grade three through secondary school.

Reimer, Wilbert and Luetta Reimer
HISTORICAL CONNECTIONS IN MATHEMATICS, Volume 1 and 2
Fresno, CA: AIMS Education Foundation, 2005
    Biographical information about twenty great mathematicians, plus portraits, illustrations, classroom-ready activities, and suggestions for use. May be reproduced. Complete solutions and a resource list. For grades 4 - 10.

Schaaf, William
MATHEMATICS AND SCIENCE: AN ADVENTURE IN POSTAGE STAMPS
Reston, Virginia: National Council of Teachers of Mathematics, 1978
    This book traces, through illustration and historical insight, the way postage stamps mirror the impact of mathematics and science on society.

The AIMS Program

AIMS is the acronym for "Activities Integrating Mathematics and Science." Such integration enriches learning and makes it meaningful and holistic. AIMS began as a project of Fresno Pacific University to integrate the study of mathematics and science in grades K-9, but has since expanded to include language arts, social studies, and other disciplines.

AIMS is a continuing program of the non-profit AIMS Education Foundation. It had its inception in a National Science Foundation funded program whose purpose was to explore the effectiveness of integrating mathematics and science. The project directors, in cooperation with 80 elementary classroom teachers, devoted two years to a thorough field-testing of the results and implications of integration.

The approach met with such positive results that the decision was made to launch a program to create instructional materials incorporating this concept. Despite the fact that thoughtful educators have long recommended an integrative approach, very little appropriate material was available in 1981 when the project began. A series of writing projects ensued, and today the AIMS Education Foundation is committed to continuing the creation of new integrated activities on a permanent basis.

The AIMS program is funded through the sale of books, products, and professional-development workshops, and through proceeds from the Foundation's endowment. All net income from programs and products flows into a trust fund administered by the AIMS Education Foundation. Use of these funds is restricted to support of research, development, and publication of new materials. Writers donate all their rights to the Foundation to support its ongoing program. No royalties are paid to the writers.

The rationale for integration lies in the fact that science, mathematics, language arts, social studies, etc., are integrally interwoven in the real world, from which it follows that they should be similarly treated in the classroom where students are being prepared to live in that world. Teachers who use the AIMS program give enthusiastic endorsement to the effectiveness of this approach.

Science encompasses the art of questioning, investigating, hypothesizing, discovering, and communicating. Mathematics is a language that provides clarity, objectivity, and understanding. The language arts provide us with powerful tools of communication. Many of the major contemporary societal issues stem from advancements in science and must be studied in the context of the social sciences. Therefore, it is timely that all of us take seriously a more holistic method of educating our students. This goal motivates all who are associated with the AIMS Program. We invite you to join us in this effort.

Meaningful integration of knowledge is a major recommendation coming from the nation's professional science and mathematics associations. The American Association for the Advancement of Science in *Science for All Americans* strongly recommends the integration of mathematics, science, and technology. The National Council of Teachers of Mathematics places strong emphasis on applications of mathematics found in science investigations. AIMS is fully aligned with these recommendations.

Extensive field testing of AIMS investigations confirms these beneficial results:

1. Mathematics becomes more meaningful, hence more useful, when it is applied to situations that interest students.
2. The extent to which science is studied and understood is increased when mathematics and science are integrated.
3. There is improved quality of learning and retention, supporting the thesis that learning which is meaningful and relevant is more effective.
4. Motivation and involvement are increased dramatically as students investigate real-world situations and participate actively in the process.

We invite you to become part of this classroom teacher movement by using an integrated approach to learning and sharing any suggestions you may have. The AIMS Program welcomes you!

AIMS Education Foundation Programs

When you host an AIMS workshop for elementary and middle school educators, you will know your teachers are receiving effective, usable training they can apply in their classrooms immediately.

AIMS Workshops are Designed for Teachers
- Correlated to your state standards;
- Address key topic areas, including math content, science content, and process skills;
- Provide practice of activity-based teaching;
- Address classroom management issues and higher-order thinking skills;
- Give you AIMS resources; and
- Offer optional college (graduate-level) credits for many courses.

AIMS Workshops Fit District/Administrative Needs
- Flexible scheduling and grade-span options;
- Customized (one-, two-, or three-day) workshops meet specific schedule, topic, state standards, and grade-span needs;
- Prepackaged four-day workshops for in-depth math and science training available (includes all materials and expenses);
- Sustained staff development is available for which workshops can be scheduled throughout the school year;
- Eligible for funding under the Title I and Title II sections of No Child Left Behind; and
- Affordable professional development—consecutive-day workshops offer considerable savings.

University Credit—Correspondence Courses
AIMS offers correspondence courses through a partnership with Fresno Pacific University.
- Convenient distance-learning courses—you study at your own pace and schedule. No computer or Internet access required!

Introducing AIMS State-Specific Science Curriculum
Developed to meet 100% of your state's standards, AIMS' State-Specific Science Curriculum gives students the opportunity to build content knowledge, thinking skills, and fundamental science processes.
- Each grade-specific module has been developed to extend the AIMS approach to full-year science programs. Modules can be used as a complete curriculum or as a supplement to existing materials.
- Each standards-based module includes mathreading, hands-on investigations, and assessments.

Like all AIMS resources, these modules are able to serve students at all stages of readiness, making these a great value across the grades served in your school.

For current information regarding the programs described above, please complete the following form and mail it to: P.O. Box 8120, Fresno, CA 93747.

Information Request

Please send current information on the items checked:

___ *Basic Information Packet* on AIMS materials
___ Hosting information for AIMS workshops
___ AIMS State-Specific Science Curriculum

Name: _____

Phone:_____ E-mail:_____

Address: _____
           Street   City   State   Zip

AIMS Magazine

YOUR K-9 MATH AND SCIENCE CLASSROOM ACTIVITIES RESOURCE

The AIMS Magazine is your source for standards-based, hands-on math and science investigations. Each issue is filled with teacher-friendly, ready-to-use activities that engage students in meaningful learning.

- *Four issues each year (fall, winter, spring, and summer).*

Current issue is shipped with all past issues within that volume.

1824	Volume XXIV	2009-2010	$19.95
1825	Volume XXV	2010-2011	$19.95

Two-Volume Combination

M20810	Volumes XXIII & XXIV	2008-2010	$34.95
M20911	Volumes XXIV & XXV	2009-2011	$34.95

Complete volumes available for purchase:

1802	Volume II	1987-1988	$19.95
1804	Volume IV	1989-1990	$19.95
1805	Volume V	1990-1991	$19.95
1807	Volume VII	1992-1993	$19.95
1808	Volume VIII	1993-1994	$19.95
1809	Volume IX	1994-1995	$19.95
1810	Volume X	1995-1996	$19.95
1811	Volume XI	1996-1997	$19.95
1812	Volume XII	1997-1998	$19.95
1813	Volume XIII	1998-1999	$19.95
1814	Volume XIV	1999-2000	$19.95
1815	Volume XV	2000-2001	$19.95
1816	Volume XVI	2001-2002	$19.95
1817	Volume XVII	2002-2003	$19.95
1818	Volume XVIII	2003-2004	$19.95
1819	Volume XIX	2004-2005	$19.95
1820	Volume XX	2005-2006	$19.95
1821	Volume XXI	2006-2007	$19.95
1822	Volume XXII	2007-2008	$19.95
1823	Volume XXIII	2008-2009	$19.95

Volumes II to XIX include 10 issues.

Call 1.888.733.2467 or go to www.aimsedu.org

Subscribe to the AIMS Magazine

$19.95 a year!

AIMS Magazine is published four times a year.

Subscriptions ordered at any time will receive all the issues for that year.

AIMS Online—www.aimsedu.org

To see all that AIMS has to offer, check us out on the Internet at www.aimsedu.org. At our website you can search our activities database; preview and purchase individual AIMS activities; learn about state-specific science, college courses, and workshops; buy manipulatives and other classroom resources; and download free resources including articles, puzzles, and sample AIMS activities.

AIMS News

While visiting the AIMS website, sign up for AIMS News, our FREE e-mail newsletter.
Included in each month's issue you will find:
- Information on what's new at AIMS (publications, materials, state-specific science modules, etc.)
- A special money-saving offer for a book and/or product; and
- Free sample activities.

Sign up today!

AIMS Program Publications

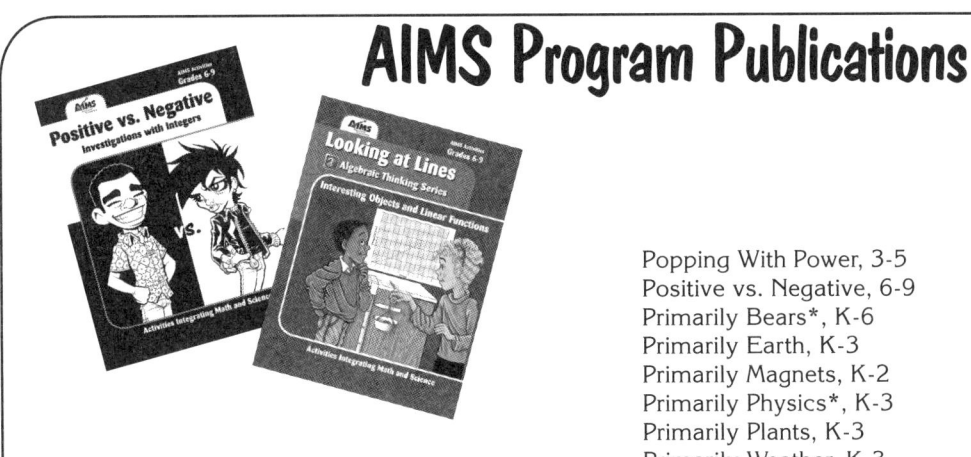

Actions with Fractions, 4-9
The Amazing Circle, 4-9
Awesome Addition and Super Subtraction, 2-3
Bats Incredible! 2-4
Brick Layers II, 4-9
The Budding Botanist, 3-6
Chemistry Matters, 4-7
Counting on Coins, K-2
Cycles of Knowing and Growing, 1-3
Crazy About Cotton, 3-7
Critters, 2-5
Earth Book, 6-9
Electrical Connections, 4-9
Exploring Environments, K-6
Fabulous Fractions, 3-6
Fall Into Math and Science*, K-1
Field Detectives, 3-6
Finding Your Bearings, 4-9
Floaters and Sinkers, 5-9
From Head to Toe, 5-9
Glide Into Winter with Math and Science*, K-1
Gravity Rules! 5-12
Hardhatting in a Geo-World, 3-5
Historical Connections in Mathematics, Vol. I, 5-9
Historical Connections in Mathematics, Vol. II, 5-9
Historical Connections in Mathematics, Vol. III, 5-9
It's About Time, K-2
It Must Be A Bird, Pre-K-2
Jaw Breakers and Heart Thumpers, 3-5
Looking at Geometry, 6-9
Looking at Lines, 6-9
Machine Shop, 5-9
Magnificent Microworld Adventures, 5-9
Marvelous Multiplication and Dazzling Division, 4-5
Math + Science, A Solution, 5-9
Mathematicians are People, Too
Mathematicians are People, Too, Vol. II
Mostly Magnets*, 3-6
Movie Math Mania, 6-9
Multiplication the Algebra Way, 6-8
Out of This World, 4-8
Paper Square Geometry:
    The Mathematics of Origami, 5-12
Puzzle Play, 4-8

Popping With Power, 3-5
Positive vs. Negative, 6-9
Primarily Bears*, K-6
Primarily Earth, K-3
Primarily Magnets, K-2
Primarily Physics*, K-3
Primarily Plants, K-3
Primarily Weather, K-3
Problem Solving: Just for the Fun of It! 4-9
Problem Solving: Just for the Fun of It! Book Two, 4-9
Proportional Reasoning, 6-9
Ray's Reflections, 4-8
Sensational Springtime, K-2
Sense-Able Science*, K-1
Shapes, Solids, and More: Concepts in Geometry, 2-3
The Sky's the Limit, 5-9
Soap Films and Bubbles, 4-9
Solve It! K-1: Problem-Solving Strategies, K-1
Solve It! 2nd: Problem-Solving Strategies, 2
Solve It! 3rd: Problem-Solving Strategies, 3
Solve It! 4th: Problem-Solving Strategies, 4
Solve It! 5th: Problem-Solving Strategies, 5
Solving Equations: A Conceptual Approach, 6-9
Spatial Visualization, 4-9
Spills and Ripples, 5-12
Spring Into Math and Science*, K-1
Statistics and Probability, 6-9
Through the Eyes of the Explorers, 5-9
Under Construction, K-2
Water, Precious Water, 4-6
Weather Sense: Temperature, Air Pressure, and Wind, 4-5
Weather Sense: Moisture, 4-5
What's Next, Volume 1, 4-12
What's Next, Volume 2, 4-12
What's Next, Volume 3, 4-12
Winter Wonders, K-2

Essential Math
Area Formulas for Parallelograms, Triangles, and Trapazoids, 6-8
Circumference and Area of Circles, 5-7
Measurement of Rectangular Solids, 5-7
The Pythagorean Relationship, 6-8

Spanish Edition
Constructores II: Ingeniería Creativa Con Construcciones
    LEGO®, 4-9
    The entire book is written in Spanish. English pages not included.

* Spanish supplements are available for these books. They are only available as downloads from the AIMS website. The supplements contain only the student pages in Spanish; you will need the English version of the book for the teacher's text.

For further information, contact:
AIMS Education Foundation • P.O. Box 8120 • Fresno, California 93747-8120
www.aimsedu.org • 559.255.6396 (fax) • 888.733.2467 (toll free)

Duplication Rights

No part of any AIMS books, magazines, activities, or content—digital or otherwise—may be reproduced or transmitted in any form or by any means—including photocopying, taping, or information storage/retrieval systems—except as noted below.

Standard Duplication Rights

- A person or school purchasing AIMS activities (in books, magazines, or in digital form) is hereby granted permission to make up to 200 copies of any portion of those activities, provided these copies will be used for educational purposes and only at one school site.
- Workshop or conference presenters may make one copy of any portion of a purchased activity for each participant, with a limit of five activities per workshop or conference session.
- All copies must bear the AIMS Education Foundation copyright information.

Standard duplication rights apply to activities received at workshops, free sample activities provided by AIMS, and activities received by conference participants.

Unlimited Duplication Rights

Unlimited duplication rights may be purchased in cases where AIMS users wish to:
- make more than 200 copies of a book/magazine/activity,
- use a book/magazine/activity at more than one school site, or
- make an activity available on the Internet (see below).

These rights permit unlimited duplication of purchased books, magazines, and/or activities (including revisions) for use at a given school site.

Activities received at workshops are eligible for upgrade from standard to unlimited duplication rights.

Free sample activities and activities received as a conference participant are not eligible for upgrade from standard to unlimited duplication rights.

State-Specific Science modules are licensed to one classroom/one teacher and are therefore not eligible for upgrade from standard to unlimited duplication rights.

Upgrade Fees

The fees for upgrading from standard to unlimited duplication rights are:
- $5 per activity per site,
- $25 per book per site, and
- $10 per magazine issue per site.

The cost of upgrading is shown in the following examples:
- activity: 5 activities x 5 sites x $5 = $125
- book: 10 books x 5 sites x $25 = $1250
- magazine issue: 1 issue x 5 sites x $10 = $50

Purchasing Unlimited Duplication Rights

To purchase unlimited duplication rights, please provide us the following:
1. The name of the individual responsible for coordinating the purchase of duplication rights.
2. The title of each book, activity, and magazine issue to be covered.
3. The number of school sites and name of each site for which rights are being purchased.
4. Payment (check, purchase order, credit card)

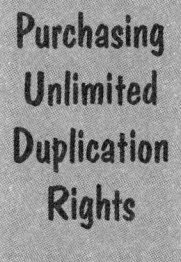

Requested duplication rights are automatically authorized with payment. The individual responsible for coordinating the purchase of duplication rights will be sent a certificate verifying the purchase.

Internet Use

AIMS materials may be made available on the Internet if all of the following stipulations are met:
1. The materials to be put online are purchased as PDF files from AIMS (i.e., no scanned copies).
2. Unlimited duplication rights are purchased for all materials to be put online for each school at which they will be used. (See above.)
3. The materials are made available via a secure, password-protected system that can only be accessed by employees at schools for which duplication rights have been purchased.

AIMS materials may not be made available on any publicly accessible Internet site.